# The Psychology of Atheism

# The Psychology of Atheism

by R.C. Sproul

Staff Theologian
Ligonier Valley Study Center

BETHANY FELLOWSHIP, INC.
Minneapolis, Minnesota

Copyright © 1974
Bethany Fellowship, Inc.
All Rights Reserved

Library of Congress Cataloging in Publication Data

Sproul, Robert Charles, 1939-
   The psychology of atheism.

   Includes bibliographical references.
   1. Apologetics—20th Century. 2. Theism.
3. Atheism. I. Title.
BT1102. S6    239'.7      74-13762
ISBN 0-87123-459-9

Bethany Fellowship, Inc.
6820 Auto Club Road, Minneapolis, Minnesota 55438
Printed in U.S.A.

To Dr. John H. Gerstner,
teacher, counselor, friend,
"a burning and a shining light"

## Table of Contents

Preface ............................... 9
1. The Great Debate ..................... 13
2. The Tension of Disagreement .......... 25
3. The Psychology of Theism ............. 41
4. The Psychology of Atheism ............ 56
5. The Trauma of Holiness ............... 81
6. God and Nakedness .................... 107
7. The Quest for Autonomy ............... 137
8. Conclusion ........................... 153
   Notes to Chapters .................... 157
   Index ................................ 165

## Preface

A chronic complaint among scholars often involves the charge that a man oversteps the bounds of his discipline by commenting on matters outside of his field. Often these complaints are valid and need to be registered. However, it is always important to remember that no major field of scholarly investigation is so specialized that it never touches other domains. Though a specialist in theology would be presumptuous to speak dogmatically about every aspect of psychological research, it would be irresponsible for him to remain silent about those aspects that touch heavily on theology. The question of man's disposition and motivation toward God is certainly of psychological import. However, it is also a question of immense theological importance. Hence this volume involves an examination of the motivating factors of the human psyche with respect to God, from a theological perspective.

A common charge leveled against people with religious beliefs in general, and with Christian convictions in particular, is that their convictions are motivated not by reasonable evidence but by psychological needs. This charge demands an *apologia* in the classical sense of the word. That is to say that the charge is worthy of a "reply." This book represents an effort to provide such an apology for Christianity. It is important to note, however, that though this book belongs to the broad category of apologetics, it does not represent a full-blown, comprehensive defense of the Christian faith. It is not my purpose to present evidence for the existence of God or to provide a total apologetic for Christianity. Rather the purpose is limited to the issue of psychological motivation. It is my contention that this issue must be dealt with before any sober analysis of the evidence for the Christian faith can be undertaken. Thus, in one sense, this book should be considered prolegomena to apologetics in the wider sense.

The central thesis of this book is this: The "attractive" features of the Christian God that might incline a person to project His existence as a bromide or narcotic to help him face the threatening character of life are not only equalized and neutralized by the threatening features of God but are overwhelmingly outweighed by the traumatic experience of encountering God. Though man may desire and create for himself a deity who meets his needs and provides him with innumerable benefits, he will not desire a God who is holy, omniscient, and sovereign.

If this book is read by one who disclaims belief in God, I can only ask for an honest and open hearing of the case. May there be a guarded truce at least until the issue of psychological projection is dealt with, that room may be provided for an open debate on the objective evidence for or against the existence of God.

Special thanks are in order for the many friends who contributed to the completion of this book. My gratitude is extended particularly to Mrs. William Chevalier, Mrs. Thomas Quarry, and Miss Mary Semach for assistance in preparing the manuscript. The reference in chapter 5 to my son's fearful departure from camping out in the woods can only be written by his permission with the proviso that I mention his recent exploit of solidly "sacking" the quarterback in a football game. Hence my allusion to his infant cowardice is now balanced by ample testimony to his incipient athletic prowess.

R. C. Sproul

The Ligonier Valley
January, 1974

CHAPTER 1

# The Great Debate

There is no perennial issue that engenders more controversy than the question of whether or not there is a God. The debate is not limited to the parlor or the marketplace, but has been the focal point of massive intellectual endeavor for millennia. The debate raged in classical antiquity as vigorously as it storms today. The Epicureans scoffed at the Stoics for their theistic assertions. The Skeptics mocked the Platonist's "Idea of the Good" and the Aristotelian's "Unmoved Mover." Not all Semitic nations were enamored or persuaded by Israel's Yahweh. In every theistic culture there have been detractors. In no sense can we say there has ever been universal acceptance of either theism or atheism.

The mode of the debate has ranged from the placid to the brutal. The Inquisition, the rack, the sword and bullet, have been utilized as means of persuasion for religious points of view. Symbolic burial of dissenting relatives has provoked "fiddling on the roof." Men fight, maim, kill, or yawn dispassionately between casual puffs of their pipes as the issue is discussed. In one culture the killing of the infidel is viewed as a work of supererrogatory merit; while another culture echos the axiom that men never should discuss religion or politics. From apathy to violence, from unbridled passion to careful, calculated reasoning, the debate takes place.

## Varieties of Theism

The word "theism" is an extremely difficult one to define. It is a generic term which incorporates a wide variety of species. Literally the word means "Godism" as it is derived from the Greek word for God, *theos*. The content of the term, however, is far more difficult to isolate than its etymological derivation. One dictionary defines theism as follows: "Belief in the existence of a god or gods."[1] If we check further in the dictionary to the entry "God," we read: "A being of more than human attributes and powers; a deity, especially a male deity; anything worshiped by man as a deity...."[2] This definition is broad in scope and serves to increase the ambiguity that so often surrounds the meaning of the word "God."

Because of the ambiguity of the word "God" and because of the multitude of meanings variously ascribed to it, many contemporary thinkers have despaired of having any meaningful discussion of the word at all (whether it, in any of its meanings, refers to something real or not). There is a conceptual and linguistic crisis in the whole area of God-talk.[3] Perhaps this can be illustrated by the now famous parable of Anthony Flew:

> "Once upon a time two explorers came upon a clearing in the jungle. In the clearing were growing many flowers and many weeds. One explorer says, 'Some gardener must tend this plot.' The other disagrees. 'There is no gardener.' So they pitch their tents and set a watch. No gardener is ever

seen. 'But perhaps he is an invisible gardener.' So they set up a barbed wire fence. They electrify it. They patrol with bloodhounds. . . . But no shrieks ever suggest that some intruder has received a shock. No movement of the wire ever betrays an invisible climber. The bloodhounds never give cry. Yet still the Believer is not convinced. 'But there is a gardener, invisible, intangible, insensible to electric shocks, a gardener who has no scent and makes no sound, a gardener who comes secretly to look after the garden which he loves.' At last the Skeptic despairs, 'But what is left of your original assertion? Just how does what you call an invisible, intangible, eternally elusive gardener differ from an imaginary gardener or even from no gardener at all?' " Flew concludes, "A fine brash of hypothesis may thus be killed by inches, the death of a thousand qualifications." [4]

In the nineteenth century, Nietszche argued that God died of pity. The contemporary mind has located the cause of death in terms of qualifications. Thus, some have concluded that the word "God" is a meaningless cipher and is incapable of usage in rational discourse. Such radical skepticism, however, is not necessitated by the problems involved. Though the word "God" abounds with linguistic difficulty, it still functions in a meaningful way in our society. Though the ideas surrounding the word are often vague and hazy, the word persists in our vocabulary.

Among the many species included in the genus, theism, are the following:

*Polytheism.* The term polytheism has specific reference to number. That is, polytheism is a variety of theism that postulates a plurality of deities. These deities often vary in gender, status, authority, and basic function and job description. The number of deities incorporated in a polytheistic schema can vary from two to infinity.

*Henotheism.* Henotheism represents a peculiar kind of theism. It is regarded as something between polytheism and monotheism but is not quite either fish or fowl. Simply stated, henotheism may be defined as geographical, ethnic, or national monotheism. That is, a particular nation or group believe in one God who reigns exclusively over them, within the context of their territorial limits. Other Gods exist and reign over other nations. Thus the existence of many gods (polytheism) is affirmed, but allegiance is given to one alone. Henotheism differs from monotheism in that the God worshiped is not cosmic in his dominion. Henotheism has also been called monolatry in that the emphasis falls to the service and or worship (latria) given to a single deity. In some cultures, henotheism represented a transitional state between the movement from polytheism to monotheism.[5]

*Monotheism.* Strictly speaking, monotheism simply refers to the belief in one cosmic deity. Radically different descriptions of that one deity may be manifested. The one deity may be regarded as personal or impersonal, transcendent or immanent, abstract or concrete, finite or infinite, etc. The term "monotheism" is usually associated in the Western World with the Judaeo-Christian tradition. However, monotheism in the sense defined is not limited to that tradition. Islam, Neo-Platonism, etc., could all be described by the broad term, "monotheism."

## Atheism and Agnosticism

*Atheism.* In a technical sense atheism is not quite as difficult to define as are the varieties of theism. Atheism involves the negation or rejection of any form of theism. To be an atheist is to disavow belief in any kind of god or gods. However, in the function of language, the term has often been employed to signify a rejection or disavowal of a particular god or group of gods: Hence in some instances the early Christians were called atheists because they rejected the popular dieties of Rome. Likewise the term atheism has been employed by many Christian thinkers in dealing with other religions. Religions that are in opposition to Christianity have been called atheistic in so far as they were understood to be worshiping false gods. This approach, whether it comes from a Christian, a Muslim, or from any other source, is usually founded on the premise that the worship of a false god is the worship of no god.

A classical example of this use of the term "atheist" can be seen in the record of the trial of the aged Bishop Polycarp as he stood in the Roman arena of the second century:

> And when finally he was brought up, there was a great tumult on hearing that Polycarp had been arrested. Therefore, when he was brought before him, the proconsul asked him if he were Polycarp. And when he confessed that he was, he tried to persuade him to deny (the faith), saying "Have respect to your age"—and other things that customarily followed this, such as, "Swear by the fortune of Caesar; change your mind; say, 'Away with the atheists!' "
>
> But Polycarp looked with earnest face at the whole crowd of lawless heathen in the arena, and motioned to them with his hand. Then groaning and looking up to heaven, he said, "Away with the atheists!" [6]

Needless to say, Polycarp burned at the stake.

*Agnosticism.* This term has more reference to a particular degree of conviction or lack of it with respect to the question of theism. Technically considered, agnosticism is a variety of atheism. If theism is considered to signify the assertion of the existence of one or more gods and a-theism means non-theism, then the agnostic is, properly speaking, an atheist. That is, if a-theism or non-theism incorporates everything outside of the category of theism, then agnosticism must be incorporated in it, insofar as it lacks any positive assertion of theism. However, the term agnosticism is rarely employed as a synonym for atheism. Rather the agnostic seeks to declare neutrality on the issue, desiring to make neither assertion nor negation of the theistic question. The term derives from the Greek *a-gnosis*, meaning without knowledge. The agnostic maintains that there is insufficient knowledge upon which to make an intellectual judgment about theism. Thus he prefers to suspend judgment until such time that more available data will incline him either to affirm or deny the existence of a god or gods.

## The Historical Situation

In terms of numerical statistics, it is safe to say that the vast majority of human beings have at least ascribed to some variety of theism. Theism has been so persistent in human civilization and has been so characteristic of man that it has been fashionable to describe man in terms of being *homo religiosus*. Man appears to be incurably religious.

As religious as the human race has manifested itself to be and as numerous as the subscribers to theism are, on the practical level the question becomes more complex. There is always a hiatus between man's profession of faith and his practice of it. Thus, it is sometimes necessary to distinguish between theoretical atheism and practical atheism.

*Practical Atheism.* Practical atheism refers to the phenomenon of people who profess belief in some kind of deity, but who, for all practical purposes, live as if there were no god. If we consider this practical dimension, perhaps the total number of "atheists" in the world (particularly in the modern world) would be substantially increased.

Countless polls have been taken in the United States to query the populace with reference to theism. Some polls have put the level of adherence to theism as high as 98%. Almost all polls have shown that a considerable majority of the American republic believe in some kind of god. Further analysis will show, however, that the god believed in is often so nebulous and ambiguous as to render the polls almost meaningless.

I witnessed a spontaneous poll of this kind administered to the studio audience of a popular television "talk show." This poll was prompted by the obvious frustration the host was experiencing with his guest. The guest was a rather well-known woman who had distinguished herself by a militant crusade against discrimination of atheists in the U.S. The host and his guest were locked in verbal combat over the issue of the existence of God. To settle the debate, the host resorted to "counting noses" to decide the issue of theism or atheism. He asked the studio audience, "How many of you believe in some kind of higher power?" The response was overwhelmingly in the affirmative. The noted guest failed to question the wording of the query. What is a "higher power"? Energy? Cosmic dust? I was left to wonder what the results of the poll would have been had it been worded differently. I wonder how the vote would have been, for example, if the question were stated, "How many of you believe in Yahweh, the God of the Old Testament Israel?"

At the practical level it makes an enormous difference whether one's god is a "studied ambiguity" such as an undefined "higher power" or is a deity with a name, a historical relationship, and content of moral imperatives. It is one thing to affirm the existence of an "unknown" god who makes no ultimate demands upon one's life; it is quite another matter to affirm the existence of a god who makes an absolute claim on life, who holds one accountable for every deed and thought, and who threatens a person with everlasting torment if he refuses to obey him.

Thus supporters of atheism can vary in number according to what kind of theism is under question.

*Modern Theoretical Atheism.* Atheism, as an intellectual option, received a great boost from the European "Aufklarung" or "Enlightenment" of the eighteenth century. This movement began in England and moved to France and then on to Germany where it found its fullest expression.

The Enlightenment has been described as a time in which all the forces of skepticism were launched against classical Christian theology. Such a description, however, would be an oversimplification and caricature of this period. The Enlightenment provoked an intense movement of intellectual analysis which opened to criticism many of the theories, opinions, and axioms of former generations in terms of psychology, historical methodology, natural science, philosophy, and theology. Indeed, every field of intellectual inquiry was touched by this movement.

One group of thinkers, within the framework of the Enlightenment, did give an emphatic critique of religion. This group was called the French Encyclopedists. Ernst Cassirer says of French Encyclopedism that it "declares war openly on religion, on its claims to validity and truth. It accuses religion of having been an eternal hindrance to intellectual progress and of having been incapable of founding a genuine morality and a just social and political order." [7]

Thus, in the minds of the Encyclopedists, a man is enlightened only when he frees himself from the God-hypothesis in order to open the way to free intellectual progress.

Perhaps the two leading voices of the French Enlightenment, in terms of atheism, were Paul Henri Thiry d'Holbach, who characterized himself as "the personal enemy of God," and Denise Diderot. Both of these thinkers approached atheism from the perspective of natural science.

Holbach argued strenuously against previous rational theories (particularly of the Cartesian school) that sought to establish the notion of God on the basis of apriori or innate knowledge. He argued that the idea of God is not innate and that the widespread belief in God among the masses does not indicate any kind of universal apriori. Holbach maintained that "the universal assent to God's existence may mean nothing more than universal terror before natural calamities together with ignorance of natural laws." [8] Notice, that in this critique of the God-hypothesis, Holbach introduces a psychological explanation as one possible explanation for the widespread belief in God. Man's terror before the unknown, and unexplained, induces him to make the gratuitous assumption that there is a god. The point Holbach makes is that with the explosion of knowledge in the areas of the natural sciences, man is liberated from the tyranny of the unknown.

Diderot shared Holbach's unbridled optimism in the natural sciences' ability to provide a basis for social, political, and moral order without recourse to a God-hypothesis. God is not a functional necessity, nor is He needed to explain the cause of the natural or moral order. Indeed, the God-hypothesis served only as a hindrance and a barrier to understanding. Both Holbach and Diderot were content with the theory of spontaneous generation to account for the origin of things and found the God-hypothesis "scientifically useless." For the Encyclopedists, the idea of God was both unnecessary and undesirable. Man and the cosmos could be adequately explained without recourse to transcendance. Consequently, a closed universe was conceived of without room for intervention from without.[9]

Though the development of the Enlightenment in Germany left its mark of criticism on Classical Christianity, it was not as hostile to theism as such as were the Encyclopedists. Lessing and Herder sought the subordination of revelation to reason; of the supernatural to the natural. Again the clarion call was to intellectual maturity, freed of dependence upon adolescent fantasies of the supernatural.

The German Enlightenment reached its zenith in the monumental work of Immanuel Kant. Kant was not an enemy of theism but rendered a serious attack on the classical arguments for the existence of God. He himself embraced a "functional theism" arguing for the existence of God on moral grounds. In spite of his own theistic position, however, Kant laid the groundwork for future rejections of the idea of God.

In his critique of the traditional arguments for the existence of God, Kant attacked the ability to move intellectually from the phenomenal realm of human experience to the noumenal world of God, the self, and the thing-in-itself. Since God, the self, and the essences are beyond the scope of empirical research they remain unknowable and undemonstrable. These noumenal ideas need to be postulated for practical purposes but cannot be verified as realities. Thus Kant could say, "We must live as though there were a God." God functions in his thought as a necessary postulate to insure a meaningful ethic.[10]

It was precisely Kant's idea of practical or functional necessity of theism that was rejected by later thinkers. If knowledge is restricted to the phenomenal realm, there is no need to go beyond that realm. The atheism that manifested itself in terms of nineteenth century thought saw no need to appeal to a noumenal being who would guarantee meaning for the phenomenal world. The leading atheists of the nineteenth century sought either to find the meaning of existence within the phenomenal world (Marx, Freud) or to reject the thesis of ultimate meaning altogether (Nietzsche).

Twentieth century atheism has followed largely along the same lines of restricting knowledge to the phenomenological realm. In both existential and analytical philosophy there has been a wholesale abandonment of metaphysical inquiry. Again, transcendental theism is viewed as being either undemonstrable or unnecessary.

## Modern Theoretical Theism

The rising crescendo of atheism established along phenomenological lines has not gone unopposed. In spite of the Enlightenment and Kant's critique of theistic proofs, theism is still very much alive. The drift of theistic belief, however, has been deeply affected by Kant's critique of rational evidence.

The dominant approach to theism in the nineteenth century manifested itself in a heavily immanentistic theology. That is, God was viewed as either part or the whole of the phenomenological realm.

This-worldliness became the arena of God rather than a remote transcendence. Revelation was largely excluded as a basis for theistic belief.

The beginning of the twentieth century saw a massive revolt against the immanentistic drift of the nineteenth century theology. The work of the Swiss theologian, Karl Barth, appeared as a protest against immanentism and a passionate defense of a deity whose transcendence is known only by revelation. Though Barth tenaciously defended a theism of transcendence, he did it within the broad context of Kant's thought. Though he argued for the validity of revelation, he acknowledged that this revelation cannot be demonstrated or authenticated by reason. Consequently theism rests, for Barth, on the foundation of faith rather than reason.[11]

This fideistic approach to theism has been widely adopted in twentieth century theology. In radically divergent views of theology, the fideistic strand remains intact. From Jasper's "Final Experience" to Bultmann's punctiliar moment of decision, to the Jesus-freaks' "mind-blowing" encounter, the emphasis falls on subjective experience as the ground-basis for theism.

Whatever the intellectual content and foundation for contemporary theism is, the fact remains that belief in God is very much a part of modern culture. Whether the foundations for theism are theoretically valid and defensible or not, the phenomenon of theism persists.

Thus, far into the twentieth century the debate between theists and atheists continues. Why? Why is there not more agreement on this vital issue? How can such brilliant thinkers and competent scholars come to such radically divergent positions?

CHAPTER 2

# The Tension of Disagreement

*Disagreement and the Law of Contradiction*

### Fact of Disagreement

We have seen from our preliminary analysis that throughout the history of Western civilization, the issue of the existence of God has not been settled once and for all. Great minds have taken opposing positions with reference to this question. Impressive arguments have come forth from the side of atheism and impressive arguments have been presented by the theists for their case. That disagreement continues is an observable fact and the issue has not been without its emotional ramifications. But disagreement has not left men in a state of dispassionate lack of concern. Rather, the debate continues, often in the context of militant polemics. Some have sought to circumvent the heat of the controversy by seeking a third alternative which would give us at least a guarded truce.

The third alternative that has captured the imagination of many contemporary Westerners is the alternative of seeing the question of the existence of God as being ultimately a subjective/practical question rather than an objective/metaphysical question. Thus, the question is dealt with on the basis of a subjective evaluation of faith or its negation. In concrete terms, a person may look at it this way: "I believe in God and that faith in God is meaningful to my human existence. It brings me comfort; it provides a goal and purpose for my life; it offers hope to me that the universe is ultimately meaningful; and because the whole of existence is ultimately meaningful, my individual life is meaningful." On the other hand, a person may say, "I do not believe in God and I've found it quite meaningful for me to live without such faith. So for me and for my life, there is no God." It is a short step for these two persons to avoid the controversy of their variant conclusions to say that for the one who finds faith meaningful, God is true and for the one who finds unbelief meaningful, God is not true.

Thus, the question of the existence of God is reduced to a question of practical meaningfulness in the life of individuals. If truth is defined as that which is meaningful to the believing subject, then of course anything that is meaningful to the subject may be regarded as true. Also, anything that is not meaningful to the subject may be regarded as false. This approach to the question of the existence of God does not alleviate the tension of disagreement. It does much to alleviate the emotional hostility that often surrounds the debate. It does much to bring us peace, but very little to bring us truth. The issue of the objective existence of God remains.

The question of God's existence is a different question from the question of what man finds meaningful and practical. By taking this third alternative, we can discover many answers to the questions of practical meaningfulness, but we will not find an answer to the question of the existence of God. For example, if I believe in God with all of my heart and with all of my mind and find that belief so meaningful that I devote my life to serving this God, if I pray to this God, if I worship this God, if I sacrifice my life to this God, and in fact there is no such God, all of my praying and devotion and sacrifice will not bring Him into existence. That is to say, if I find all kinds of subjective practical meaning by believing in God, that meaningfulness will not cause a God to be, apart from me, if in fact there is no such God apart from me. On the other hand, if I do not believe in God and am convinced that God is the invention of superstitious minds, is an unintellectual proposition, and is irrelevant to my existence; if I find my meaning in life without reference to God and in fact there is a God apart from me, all of my unbelief and unconcern and disinterest will not change that fact. In the final analysis there either is a God or Gods or there are none. There either is something or someone ultimate apart from me or there is not.

Not only can the question of the objective existence of God not be decided by subjective meaningfulness of the individual, but the question can also not be decided by a collective discovery of subjective meaningfulness of the God-hypothesis. That is to say, my individual belief or lack of it cannot decide the ultimate question of the existence of God nor can a number of individual beliefs decide the ultimate issue. Simply stated, truth is not determined by "counting noses." Such a democratic approach to truth wherein the majority wins can again only be descriptive of what the many believe rather than what actually is. If 99% of the people of the world believes in God, that does not mean there is a God. Conversely, if 99% of the world believes there is no God, that in itself does not decide the issue. Five thousand Frenchmen can be wrong.

## The Law of Contradiction

In the objective realm of the question of the existence of God both sides cannot be right. There cannot be a God or Gods on the one hand and at the same time be no Gods. To avoid the pain of disagreement by affirming both poles is to violate the law of contradiction. Formally stated, the law of contradiction is that A cannot be A and non-A at the same time. That is to say, there cannot be God and no God at the same time. To say that God is altogether and is not altogether is to say nothing ultimately. To be sure, the twentieth century has manifested a fascinating tendency to ignore the law of contradiction as a necessary principle for coherent and meaningful discourse. In reaction against previous forms of rationalism, many contemporary thinkers, particularly of the existentialist school, have maintained that truth indeed may be contradictory; that truth transcends logical categories and cannot be conceived of in terms of the law of contradiction. On the other hand, thinkers who have persisted to operate within the framework of the law of contradiction have been charged with perpetuating an Aristotelian system of truth that can no longer function in the context of the modern thought.

It should be made emphatically clear that adherence to the law of contradiction in meaningful discourse does not presuppose a passive acceptance of the Aristotelian metaphysic or the Aristotelian epistemology. Aristotle did not invent logic, nor was the law of contradiction the conclusion of his system.

For Aristotle, logic was defined, not invented. He described logic as being the *organon* of all science. That is, logic was viewed as a necessary instrument or tool by which knowledge could be coherently expressed and understood.[1] Statements that violated the law of contradiction were judged by Aristotle to be nonsense statements, to be meaningless with respect to content.

Though in the twentieth century we have seen a wholesale rejection of the law of contradiction at the theoretical level, we have seen at the same time a virtual universal acceptance of the law of contradiction at the practical level. That is to say, that though many deny the validity of the law of contradiction intellectually, they all live their daily lives in the tacit assumption of the validity of the law. For example, the existential philosopher who denies the validity of the law of contradiction, under normal circumstances will not drive his car through an intersection of a highway, having seen that a very large truck is speeding towards the point of the intersection where he wishes to proceed. He stops his car because he knows that if there is a truck in front of him there cannot at the same time not be a truck in front of him. As he thinks his theory of non-contradiction, he applies the brakes in his car. If a doctor found conclusive evidence for the presence of a malignant cancer in the body of one of his patients and reasoned within himself that there was also no cancer in his patient's body and treated the patient on the basis of that possibility, his treatment would be regarded as nothing less than criminal. Man cannot survive or function without assuming the validity of the law of contradiction.

In the intellectual community there is often a profound fascination with statements that are made that are blatant violations of the law of contradiction.

At first impact, such statements from intelligent professors often carry the aura of profundity and produce a sense of awe in the mind of the bewildered student. For example, I once witnessed a well-known theologian making the statement to his students that "God is absolutely immutable in his essence: God is absolutely mutable in his essence." At the end of such a blatantly contradictory statement, the professor paused to allow his words to sink in. The reaction of his students was almost reverential. They were filled with a sense of awe at the depths of the professor's profundity. When I queried some of the students as to what they learned from such a statement, they admitted that they had learned nothing, but that the professor's statement was certainly deep and penetrating. One student remarked, "I cannot understand what the professor was saying. It is too deep for me, but I am sure the professor must understand it because he is so much more brilliant than I."

A further example may be drawn from my own experience as a professor of philosophy. On one occasion I stood before my class and held a piece of chalk in my hand. I said to the students, which included on that particular afternoon the dean of the school as he sat in to audit my class, "This piece of chalk is not a piece of chalk." I made the statement in a tone of voice that was somewhat hushed and awe-inspired, the kind of voice a professor might use when he is trying to communicate something penetratingly deep. I screwed up my face and my forehead to make myself appear contemplative and pensive. After the statement was made, I asked the students, "What did you learn from that statement?" After some careful consideration one student answered the query by saying, "That piece of chalk is not really a piece of chalk." I responded, "What piece of chalk?" and the student said, "*That* piece of chalk." I said, "But this piece of chalk in not a piece of chalk, so why do you call it a piece of chalk?" At this point the student became befuddled and an atmosphere of confusion permeated the room. After a further period of silent contemplation, the dean became involved in the inquiry by stating, "I have learned that that *particular* piece of chalk which you have in your hand is not a piece of chalk." I said, "Which particular piece of chalk?" He indicated the piece of chalk I had in my hand and I replied, "I told you this piece of chalk is not a piece of chalk. Why do you insist on calling it a piece of chalk?" Finally, after much frustration that was moving toward the level of annoyance, an auditing student who was a Negro of middle age could stand the intellectual nonsense no longer, boldly declared, "Man, I ain't learned nothin'!" Needless to say, I was relieved to discover that there was at least one sentient creature left in the room. Thus, in some circumstances the bold declaration and profession of both sides of a contradiction may sound clever or profound, but upon closer scrutiny finally yield to its absurdity.

The law of contradiction is not a system of truth, it is not a self-contained philosophy, it is not even an epistemology. It is simply what Artistotle called it—an organ of meaningful discourse; an instrument necessary for verbal communication to be understood. The law of contradiction cannot, in and of itself, prove the existence of God nor, of course, could it disprove the existence of God. The service rendered to us at this point by the law of contradiction is simply this: that it demonstrates to us that we cannot solve the tension of disagreement by affirming both poles. One side must be wrong, both sides cannot be right. A flight into a subjective *tertium quid* only adds to the dilemma of the classical issue. Thus the disagreement remains, and we move then to the question of why the disagreement remains. How is it possible for men of equal brilliance, of equal intellectual prowess, indeed of equal educational backgrounds and sophistication to arrive at two mutually exclusive disparate conclusions?

## Reasons for Disagreement About Objective Truth

When experts disagree and come to mutually exclusive conclusions, a normal tendency of the layman is to assume that the problem is insoluble. In reality however, it is quite possible that one set of conclusions may in fact be correct while the other is in error. It is also possible that the expert who comes to the right conclusion has come to that conclusion as much through good fortune as through good reasoning. That is to say, it is possible that the expert who has come to the wrong conclusion has been more consistent in his reasoning than the expert who arrives at the correct conclusion. Be that as it may, the fact that experts disagree does not mean that a question is insoluble. The obvious reason is, of course, because experts are capable of making mistakes. The greatest minds are subject to error. There are innumerable ways in which errors can be and are made in the process of rational debate. A considerable number of factors may be involved that will lead to error. For purposes of simplification, we can elucidate four basic kinds of errors that are frequently made by the greatest of men. The four ways in which errors can be made and by which disagreement comes are the following:

1. Epistemological errors
2. Formal errors in reasoning
3. Factual errors in empirical investigation
4. Psychological prejudice that distorts conclusions

*Epistemological Variants*

Epistemology is that branch of philosophy that deals specifically with the question of knowledge. It deals with definition of truth and methodology of attaining truth. There is no universally accepted epistemology by which experts operate. Classically, there have been many schools of epistemology, the most famous of which have been the schools of rationalism and empiricism. The various schools of rationalism have given great emphasis to the function of reasoning in order to arrive at truth. The accent has fallen upon the formal and theoretical rather than upon the material and the empirical. In extreme cases some from the tradition of rationalism argued that whatever can be conceived as being true logically must exist in reality. We can call this school the conceptualist school. That which can be conceived by the mind in rational categories must exist in reality. The seventeenth century essentialists were representative of this approach to truth.

On the other hand, the empiricist has sought to discover truth more through the process of sense perception than through local speculation. Over against the idea that whatever can be *conceived* as being truth is true is the notion that whatever is *perceived* by the senses is true. Whatever cannot be perceived by the senses is not true. Thus, two experts using these two vastly different approaches to knowledge could easily come to variant conclusions regarding the question of the existence of God.

The conceptualist might argue that to conceive of God is perfectly proper within the context of rational speculation and does not pose immediate problems of irrationality and therefore must be regarded as being true.[2] On the other hand, one who followed a very strict empirical course of epistemology would argue that a metaphysical being called God whose essence cannot be known empirically and perceived by the senses cannot be true because it cannot meet the test for truth, that of empirical verification.[3]

Thus we can see how two brilliant minds can come to disparate conclusions using two variant epistemologies as their basis for investigation. Of course it is important to remember that the two epistemologies mentioned above are by no means the only epistemologies vying for acceptance among scholars. Indeed it would be very unlikely to find many philosophers in the twentieth century who would take such a one-sided view of rationalism or such a one-sided view of empiricism as outlined above. Thus, the conclusion of the theist or the atheist may be largely conditioned by the validity or invalidity of the epistemology employed.

## *Formal Errors*

It must be maintained that even if a philosopher uses a perfectly valid epistemology, that will be no guarantee that the conclusions of his thought will be equally valid. Though the starting point may be correct, it is quite possible that errors of reasoning may occur throughout the process of the thought. Though not all philosophers have been rationalists, all philosophers have resorted to some kind of reasoning process in articulating their various views. This has been made manifest and demonstrated in existential philosophy as well as other forms of epistemology.

The question of formal truth concerns the question of internal consistency. It involves questions of logic and of statements that can be verified or falsified strictly on a formal basis. For example, if a philosopher began with the statement, "All men are mortal," and used that as his first premise, then inductively came to the conclusion of the second premise, namely, that Socrates was a man, and stated for his conclusion that therefore Socrates was not a mortal, this would give obvious evidence of a logical fallacy that has been made. It is interesting that in logic courses at the university level dealing with such formal questions and dealing with examples of fallacies, students are often presented with passages taken not from the lower classes of literature, such as comic books or tabloids or propaganda manuscripts, but from the finest literary products of western culture. Passages from John Stuart Mill, David Hume, Immanuel Kant, Aristotle, Cicero, etc., are used as illustrations of examples of blatant logical fallacies present in the works of the most learned men.[4]

Thus, another reason why brilliant men disagree about very important issues is because brilliant men are capable of making formal mistakes in their reasoning process. Thus when we see experts disagree, we must not assume at the outset that the experts in question have all been consistently reasonable in their formal argumentation.

## Factual or Inductive Errors

Just as men can err in formal reasoning, so can mistakes creep into our thinking by virtue of errors made in collection of data inductively and empirically. Descartes in his day demonstrated the very real possibility of perception errors made by men. We are aware of the limitations of our sense organs to grant us total knowledge and accuracy. For example, there are frequencies of sound which are so high that they are not audible under normal circumstances for the human ear. This was made painfully aware to me in an incident from my childhood. Having purchased a new puppy, I went to the hardware store to buy a new dog whistle. Upon coming home I tested the whistle by blowing it, but I heard no sound. I returned to the store and complained that the whistle did not work and asked for a refund of my money. It was then that the store owner carefully explained to me that though I could not hear the sound of the whistle, my young puppy could and would respond. That was my practical introduction to the difference of sensitivity of perceiving sound between the human ear and the ear of a dog.

The other senses that we possess are also seen to be less in strength and sensitivity than other creatures in our own environment. There are animals whose sense of smell is considerably greater than ours, others whose sense of sight is greater, etc. We have been able to overcome some of the limitations of our senses by the invention of extremely critical and sophisticated and sensitive machinery of measurement and observation. But even these machines cannot be claimed to offer perfect sense perception. These natural limits will always be involved in the empirical process.

Not only are we materially vulnerable to the limits of our sensibilities, but we always face the problem of reaching conclusions on the basis of insufficient data. For example, if a hundred college students participated in a dormitory meal and thirty of those students were immediately affected by food poisoning, we would seek to find the common denominator in their experience in order to isolate the cause of their sickness. If we discovered that seventy of the students had lemon meringue pie for dessert and the other thirty students had cherry pie for dessert and that it was the students that had the cherry pie that were sick, we would be strongly inclined to come to the conclusion that the cherry pie was the cause of the food poisoning.

Suppose, however, the real cause of the sickness was the fact that the waitress who administered the cherry pie to all the people who came in that particular line was carrying a highly infectious and contagious disease and that in fact the cause of the illness was not the cherry pie, but rather the cherry pie was simply the avenue by which these thirty people came in contact with the real cause of the disease. To simply stop at the cherry pie would be to come to a conclusion with insufficient evidence.

The problem of empirical error is complicated in the realm of negation of existence. In a certain sense, it would be easier to verify the existence of something empirically than to negate the existence of something empirically. For example, if one made the assertion that there was gold in Alaska, the verification of that statement could conceivably be done very quickly and very simply. Though unlikely, it would be possible that the first spade of earth overturned in Alaska would produce gold. If such a happening took place, the original assertion would be verified. However, to negate the assertion empirically that there is gold in Alaska would involve searching every square inch of that land to finally say with certainty there was no gold in Alaska.

Because of this differential of facility of verification, many theists have taken comfort and consolation that empirically speaking it's virtually impossible to disprove the existence of God. For to do so would involve a thorough investigation empirically of every nook and cranny of the entire universe. The atheist of course has pointed out that he is not seeking to deny the existence of God merely on the basis of empirical data, but is arguing that the assertion of the existence of God leaves the onus of the burden of proof upon the affirmer rather than upon the denier at least from an empirical perspective.

Another subtle problem with inductive research and human fallibility was pointed out in the early stages of the LSD controversy. When a wave of protest arose concerning the experiments conducted by Dr. Timothy Leary at Harvard University, Leary was charged with the improper use of hallucinogenic drugs. Leary responded to the charges by arguing that LSD was not an "hallucinogenic" drug but rather a "psychedelic" drug. Thus a word was coined that became a staple word in popular jargon that could not be found in the 1956 edition of *Webster's New Collegiate Dictionary.*

What was Leary's point? His key argument was that a hallucinogenic drug was a drug that effected a distorted view of reality. Hallucinations involve delusions. On the other hand, claimed Leary, LSD effected not an illusory view of reality but a heightened ability to perceive reality. LSD was not mind-distorting, but mind-expanding. He cited the testimonies of numerous personages from the artistic world to buttress his claim. Artists told of being more acutely aware of color and texture while under the influence of the drug. Musicians claimed to be able to perceive previously unknown harmonics. People involved in the sex-revolution issued claims that LSD so increased tactile sensitivity that users were able to experience orgasms in their elbows.

Who was able to gainsay these claims? At a practical and ultimately a legal level, Leary was raising afresh the old philosophical dilemma of subject/ object. The issue of primary and secondary qualities which preoccupied the minds of the British Empiricists raised its head again in the LSD controversy. Thus the empirical, inductive method is haunted by the question of the limitations of our sensory organs and the question of how much the subject imposes on the data he is investigating.

## *Psychological Prejudice*

This fourth category of causal factors for error looms as a constant threat to accurate conclusions. If a man's epistemological system is sound, his deductive reasoning impeccable, and his inductive procedure inerrant, all of this would not guarantee proper conclusions. By reason of emotional bias he might still refuse to yield to the obvious conclusion of his research. Archie Bunkerism is not limited to a television situation-comedy. A classic aphorism of our culture is "a man convinced against his will, holds his original belief still." This emotional tenacity to persevere in an opinion against all evidence is humorously illustrated by an anecdote related by the Lutheran theologian, John Warwick Montgomery. Montgomery tells his modern parable:

> Once upon a time (note the mystical cast) there was a man who thought he was dead. His concerned wife and friends sent him to the friendly neighborhood psychiatrist. The psychiatrist determined to cure him by convincing him of one fact that contradicted his belief that he was dead. The fact the psychiatrist decided to use was the simple truth that dead men do not bleed. He put his patient to work reading medical texts, observing autopsies, etc. After weeks of effort the patient finally said, "All right, all right! You've convinced me. Dead men do not bleed." Whereupon the psychiatrist

stuck him in the arm with a needle, and the blood flowed. The man looked down with a contorted, ashen face and cried: "Good Lord! Dead men bleed after all!" [5]

Emotional prejudice is not limited to the dull-witted, the illiterate and poorly educated. It is exceedingly difficult for the most brilliant of men to be free of it. Philosophers and theologians are not exempt from vested interests and psychological prejudice that distort thinking.

The purpose of the foregoing survey of error-factors is not to build a foundation for despair or provide a basis for resigned skepticism. Though the road to knowledge may be fraught with perils of error, it is a road that must be taken if we are to think at all. To be aware of the possibility of prejudice, or even of its clear existence is not to cure it but that awareness is a prerequisite for the cure.

The question of the existence of God is a question that provokes deep emotional and psychological prejudice. In the arena of theological-philosophical debate the stands are crowded with vested interest. It is precisely this dimension of psychological vested interest that has been the impetus for much speculation concerning the origin of religious belief.

## CHAPTER 3

# The Psychology of Theism

Psychological prejudice may distort our reasoning with reference to many controversial issues. Perhaps there is no issue more vulnerable to the intrusion of prejudice than the issue of religion. We know that questions of religion touch virtually every aspect of our existence. Individuals' relationships to their families, their societies, and their cultures are often carried out in the midst of religious questions. The Orthodox Jew who leaves his tradition to marry a Gentile feels the pressure of religious questions. The Roman Catholic who practices birth control feels the weight of ecclesiastical censure. Even the "liberated" prostitute discovers conflicts with her culture. Xaviera Hollander, the famous New York ex-madame, screams to the world of her happiness as a "hooker," but a bit too loudly. Professing a freedom from sexual frigidity or inhibition, she nevertheless reveals that her uninhibited performance is diminished when placed against a background of church music.

Blaise Pascal touched the nerve of the issue in his now classic definition of man as paradox. Man finds himself suspended between the poles of infinity and nothingness, having the body of a beast and the mind of an angel. Man is acutely aware of his contingency as he experiences the threat of nothingness. A grain of sand in the kidney of Oliver Cromwell can change the destiny of a nation. Man is caught in the paradox of being at the same time *homo grandeur* and *homo misere.* Man's *grandeur* is located in the ability to contemplate his own existence. But this grandeur is at the same time misery as man can contemplate a better existence than he presently enjoys. Yet he is never able to actualize the possibilities he contemplates.[1]

It is precisely this ability to contemplate a better existence that lies behind most psychological theories for the origin of religion. The threat of extinction or of nothingness provokes a projected wish for a future existence that is better than the one we now enjoy or endure. The notion of heaven where there will be no death, no pain, no suffering, no tears, and no darkness can be enormously appealing to a miserable man.

### Freud's Analysis of Religion

Freud was a convinced atheist as well as being an astute observer and analyst of human beings. Like many other thinkers of the post-Enlightenment situation, he wrestled with the question, "If there is no god, why is there religion?" Freud looked not to textbooks on religion but to the complexities of the human psyche for the answer to that question.

Freud points to the restrictions imposed on individuals by civilization as a critical factor in the emergence of religion. In a society composed of individuals, restrictions of private desires are necessary for mutual survival. Without societal restrictions man is left in the brutal state of nature where only the strong, indeed the strongest, can survive. In the face of the threat of nature, society is born. "The principal task of civilization, its actual raison d'etre, is to defend us against nature."[2] However, even civilization, no matter how well advanced, cannot totally vanquish the threat of nature.

> There are the elements, which seem to mock at all human control: the earth, which quakes and is torn apart and buries all human life and its works; water, which deluges and drowns everything in a turmoil; storms, which blow everything before them; there are diseases, which we have only recently recognized as attacks by other organisms; and finally there is the painful riddle of death, against which no medicine has yet been found, nor probably will be. With these forces nature rises up against us, majestic, cruel and inexorable; she brings to our mind once more our weakness and helplessness, which we thought to escape through the work of civilization.[3]

If civilization cannot control nature and remove its threat, what can? The answer, of course, is the projection of religious character to nature itself. Freud sees the first step being the *humanization* of nature. Freud says:

> Impersonal forces and destinies cannot be approached; they remain eternally remote. But if the elements have passions that rage as they do in our own souls, if death itself is not something spontaneous but the violent act of an evil Will, if everywhere in nature there are Beings around us of a kind that we know in our own society, then we can breathe freely, can feel at home in the uncanny and can deal by psychical means with our senseless anxiety. We are still defenseless, perhaps, but we are no longer helplessly paralysed; we can at least react.[4]

Thus, once nature is humanized or personalized the possibility of psychical reaction is insured. Persons can be dealt with in a way impersonal forces cannot. If nothing else, persons can be appeased.

Freud traces the development of religion from a simplistic animism to a complex monotheism which culminates in a benevolent Providence who manifests father-like characteristics. Once God becomes a single person, "man's relations to him could recover the intimacy and intensity of the child's relation to his father." [5]

The father-image of God is also relevant to the origin of religion as it relates to the phenomenon of guilt. Both in *Totem and Taboo* and in *Civilization and its Discontents* Freud articulates his hypothesis of a primordial tribal struggle between the Father-chief and the young sons which culminated in the murder of the Father. This deed leaves the young men with tormented consciences which are only relieved by the worship and appeasement of the now deified image of the departed "Father." Thus, between the humanization of nature and the psychic responses to ambivalent feelings men have toward their fathers, Freud presents a psychological basis for the phenomenon of religion. Fear of nature and guilt toward father comprise a formidable tandem for religious belief and practice.[6]

## Ludwig Feuerbach

Ludwig Feuerbach presented the nineteenth century with a classical critique of both religion in general and Christianity in particular. Feuerbach's basic thesis is that "Religion is the dream of the human mind." [7] He sees theology as being in the final analysis nothing more than anthropology. Man's deities are merely the projected images of himself produced by a highly active imagination. Religion, says Feuerbach, has its basis in the essential difference between man and brute—the brutes have no religion.

Man has religion because he has self-consciousness and the ability to abstract and project his abstractions to the ideal form. God is the projection of Absolute Personality. This god is important to man as he provides a means to reach the goal of immortality. Death is the catalyst for religion. If there would be no death there would be no religion. For Feuerbach, the resurrection of Christ is seen as "the realized wish of man to immediate certainty of his personal continuity of existence." [8] Feuerbach maintains that religion expresses the human attempt of apotheosis or self-deification. Man's images of God are always anthropomorphic.

> Such as are a man's thoughts and dispositions, such is his God; so much worth as a man has, so much and no more has his God. Consciousness of God is self-consciousness, knowledge of God is self-knowledge. By his God thou knowest the man, and by the man his God; the two are identical.[9]

Feuerbach goes on to indicate that man's images of his gods vary from culture to culture and inevitably take on characteristics of the culture. The ancient Germans had a god who was a supreme warrior; the Homeric gods were dominated by Zeus because Zeus was the strongest of the gods and physical strength was an exalted quality of the Homeric age. Caucasian cultures have white deities; negroid cultures have black ones. Indian gods look and act like Indians and cowboy gods look and act like cowboys. Man's deities express his egoism. He goes on to say, "If the plants had eyes, taste, and judgment, each plant would declare its own flower the most beautiful." [10] Thus, what man is not, but what he wills to be or wishes to be, just that and only that, nothing else, is God.

## Karl Marx

Marx was interested in the phenomenon of religion not for metaphysical reasons but rather for reasons that related to his broader dialectical understanding of history. Picking up where Feuerbach left off, Marx leveled a critique of religion that has its roots in egoism and phantasy. Man seeks a superman who mirrors himself. Religion creates the phantasy which provides man with comfort, with an opium for the masses.[11]

Marx sees the origin of religion as a peculiar manifestation of the class struggle. Religious doctrines are but human fabrications invented by the ruling class for the purpose of economic exploitation. To be sure, this exploitation is not blatant, but veiled in religious guise. The poor worker is told by the "religious" ruler that poverty is a virtue. The gods are offered as the bearers of future euphoria. The land beyond "Jordan" is promised to the productive and obedient slaves. While the poor man looks for his reward in heaven, the ruling class is getting rich at his present expense. The worker loses his material goods but keeps his soul intact for the future. Thus, religion serves as a necessary tool to keep the workers from revolution. Marx writes:

> In the conditions of the proletariat, those of old society at large are already virtually swamped. The proletarian is without property; his relation to his wife and children has no longer anything in common with the bourgeois family-relations; modern industrial labor, modern subjugation to capital, the same in England as in France, in America as in Germany, has stripped him of every trace of national character. Law, morality, *religion* are to him so many bourgeois prejudices, behind which lurk in ambush just as many bourgeois interests.[12]

Thus, for Marx, religion is due to the creative imagination of a particular segment of mankind. Religion is utilized by the bourgeois to protect themselves from a "natural" fear, the fear of a prolatariat revolution.

## Nietzsche

Frederick Nietzsche sees religion having its roots in man's fear of facing the struggles of being locked in combat resulting from mutual lust-for-power. Religion provides a basis for morality which in turn keeps the potential "Superman" in check. In *Beyond Good and Evil*, Nietzsche distinguishes between what he calls a "slave morality" and a "master morality." The slave embraces a morality that exalts his own weakness and the master espouses a morality that exalts his own power. In terms of slave or "herd" morality Nietzsche writes:

> Those qualities which serve to alleviate the existence of sufferers are brought into prominence and flooded with light; it is here that sympathy, the kind, helping hand, the warm heart, patience, diligence, humility, and friendliness attain to honor; for here these are the most useful qualities, and almost the only means of supporting the burden of existence. Slave morality is essentially the morality of utility.[13]

Nietzsche saw in Christianity the epitome of slave morality manifesting itself. He saw Christendom (particularly as it was manifested in Nineteenth Century Europe) as the symbol of the complete destruction of natural values. Christianity is the negation and devaluation of all that is natural. It is the mortal enemy of natural ethics.[14] Religion is invented by weak men who cannot face a universe where there are no ultimate goals, no ultimate truths, no ultimate meaning. Religion signifies the victory of Apollo over Dionysus and the loss of man's heroic consciousness. He says:

> Behold, I teach you the Superman. The Superman is the meaning of the earth. Let your will say: the Superman shall be the meaning of the earth! I entreat you, my brothers, remain true to the earth, and do not believe those who speak to you of superterrestrial hopes! They are poisoners, whether they know it or not.[15]

Thus, according to Nietzsche religion perseveres because men need it. He says concerning Christianity:

> Most people in old Europe, as it seems to me, still need Christianity at present, and on that account it still finds belief. For such is man: a theological dogma might be refuted to him a thousand times, provided, however, that he had need of it, he again and again accepts it as "true,"—according to the famous "proof of power" of which the Bible speaks.[16]

Thus, in these men (Freud, Feuerbach, Marx, and Nietzsche) we have but a few examples of great thinkers who have located the "whence" of religion in one aspect of man's psychological make-up or the other. Fear of nature, wish-projection, relief from guilt and anxiety, fear of economic revolution, and fear of the nihil are all various expressions of psychological states within man that make the idea of religion an appealing matter. To be left alone and unprotected in a hostile or indifferent universe is a terrifying thought. Thus, the proverbial maxim "necessity is the mother of invention" is applied to religion as well as to myriad drugs or television sets.

From the contemporary perspective, Bertrand Russell has recapitulated the wish-projection motif as the answer to the question of the origin of religion. He says in his essay "Why I am not a Christian":

> Religion is based, I think, primarily and mainly upon fear. It is partly the terror of the unknown and partly, as I have said, the wish to feel that you have a kind of elder brother who will stand by you in all your troubles and disputes. Fear is the basis of the whole thing—fear of the mysterious, fear of defeat, fear of death. Fear is the parent of cruelty, and therefore it is no wonder if cruelty and religion have gone hand in hand. It is because fear is at the basis of those two things. In this world we can now begin a little to understand things, and a little to master them by help of science, which has forced its way step by step against the Christian religion, against the churches, and against the opposition of all the old precepts. Science can help us to get over this craven fear in which mankind has lived for so many generations. Science can teach us, and I think our own hearts can teach us, no longer to look around for imaginary supports, no longer to invent allies in the sky, but rather to look to our own efforts here below to make this world a fit place to live in, instead of the sort of place that the churches in all these centuries have made it.[17]

Any one of these psychological projections might possibly explain the origin of religion. To prove that they did, however, is a formidable task. The question of the origin of religion cannot be settled ultimately by either the psychologist or the philosopher. The question of the origin of religion is a question of history, not of psychology and philosophy. The psychologist may present data for our consideration as to what the human psyche can and does like to project and offer a multitude of possible psychological reasons why men might invent religion. But to show what men *can* do and *might* do is not to show what men *did* do. To prove that a man is capable of murder is insufficient evidence to convict a man of the fact of murder. Though it is helpful to demonstrate a murder suspect had a motive for committing the crime, it does not prove that he committed the crime.

We must be careful to note that the foregoing arguments and/or theories can never be used as proof for the nonexistence of God. They can indeed be useful to counter the argument of the theist that states the only possible explanation for the phenomenon of religion is the existence of God. Such an argument could be countered very nicely by the theories mentioned in this chapter.

Nor is there any real attempt to disprove the existence of God by men like Freud, Marx, *et al.*, by means of the theories mentioned. Their arguments already presuppose the nonexistence of God. They are not dealing with the question "Is there a God?" They are dealing with the question, "Since there is no God, why is there religion?" If in fact there is no God, their research is valuable to our understanding of man and the phenomenon of religion. The issue of theism/atheism is not over the question "Why does man believe in God?" The ultimate issue is not why do men fear the contingencies of their existence, but rather why are there contingent beings in a contingent universe worrying about the problems of contingency?

To show demonstrably that men desire a God or have a propensity to wish for the existence of a deity is not to demonstrate anything about whether or not there is, in fact, such a deity that corresponds to their desires. Unless we can establish a universal principle to the effect that anything man desires to be cannot or does not exist, the above explanations do not touch on the issue of the existence of God.

These are phenomenological analyses that begin and end on the phenomenological level. They may teach us much concerning *man*, but say nothing with respect to God.

Again, if the only argument the theist can proffer for the existence of God is the widespread phenomenon of religion and maintains further that the only possible explanation for the origin of religion is the existence of God, then of course, Marx, Freud, and the others have dealt a serious blow to the cause of theism. Certainly the theist would be somewhat embarrassed if there were no such thing as religious phenomena. If he argued for the existence of a God in whom no one believed and could point to no evidence of religious phenomena that indicated some sort of human response to the deity it would be a bit embarrassing. However much embarrassment that would cause, it would not be ultimately destructive of his position. The absence of religion might push the theist into a situation of loneliness, but not to theoretical and intellectual defeat.

It is necessary to point out that classical theism by no means rests its case for the existence of God on the phenomenon of religion. It is comforting to the theist that he is preserved from loneliness in the context of religion, but in terms of the debate, religion serves as at best corrobative evidence for his faith, not compelling evidence. If the atheist could show that the *only* evidence for the existence of God that theists can offer is religious phenomena, then again a serious blow would be dealt to the theist.

It is also very important to note that what Freud and others offer are plausible alternate explanations to the origin of religion other than those offered by theists. It is one thing to demonstrate that man *can* fabricate religious experiences; it is another thing to demonstrate that he *did*. It is one thing to argue that men *can* invent religion out of psychological necessity; it is another to argue that he did. The former involves questions of psychological and intellectual ability, the latter, questions of history. When Freud speaks of *origins*, he is writing as a historian, not as a psychologist. We know his competence as a psychologist; his competence as a historian is certainly not as well attested.

It is somewhat fascinating to the theist that the now traditional explanations for the origin of religion offered by atheists are inseparably tied to a principle of causality. Why are atheists even bothered with giving a causal explanation for religion? This is fascinating and ironic for historical reasons. When we see one of the critical contributing factors to the breakdown of the traditional proofs for the existence of God was the factor of skepticism with respect to causality, introduced by Hume and never overcome by Kant, we wonder about the implications of reintroducing the principle to explain religion. If the atheist can live intellectually with massive causeless effect such as the material universe, why is he constrained to provide a cause for such a small thing as religion?

## Freud

Freud has been very helpful to the intellectual world in showing that man has a dimension of religious desire. He has been even more helpful in relating the phenomenon of guilt to that dimension of religious consciousness. Surely nature is threatening to man and produces anxiety, fear, etc. Surely the threat of nature is indeed reduced by humanizing and personalizing it. Surely religion does offer a soothing comfort in light of that threat and stands as a highly desirable option to that threat. All of this may be true, but it would involve a gratuitous leap of the highest magnitude to conclude from this that there is no comforting reality such as God in the universe. I am not accusing Freud of making that gratuitous leap, but countless thousands of people have and continue to do so. A benevolent Father may be an attractive incitement to religious devotion. On the other hand, an angry father may be equally inciting to move toward atheism. Freud himself candidly admitted that an unpleasant experience he suffered in an encounter with his own father may have predisposed him toward feelings of antipathy to "Father-Gods."

### Feuerbach

Like Freud, Feuerbach has contributed considerable insight into human religious phenomena. He has called attention to the fact that men have a proclivity for portraying their gods in their own image, giving to their deities characteristics and attributes of themselves. That men are prone to fashion religious idols in their own image is no surprise to the Christian. That human pride and arrogance manifest themselves in human religious practices, art, etc., should be carefully noted by every theist. But again, Feuerbach's analysis teaches us much about man, but precious little about the existence or nonexistence of God.

### Marx

Marx's critique of religion has great value not only for the atheist but the theist as well. At the point of demonstrating the use of religion to manipulate and exploit the poor and oppressed of this world, Marx has been virtually prophetic. His insights into the dimensions of labor and economics are of lasting value. Since Marx, no one can afford to ignore the fact that man's labor has much to do with man's existence and history. Surely it is evident that religion has all too often served as a bromide or opium for the masses, and a tool of exploitation for the rich. As devastating as Marx's critique of religion is, however, it adds nothing to the question of the existence of God. Most religions and especially Christianity are quick to admit that religion and religious institutions are given to exploitation and manipulation and a host of other evils and admit that they are in great fear of ultimately facing nothing less than the unmitigated wrath of God for that fact. But again, a corporate socio-economic explanation for the origin of religion *may* be the correct one but has not yet been demonstrated that it *is* the correct one. That man can invent a god for socio-economic reasons is not to demonstrate that he has. Or if it can be shown that some or even most men "invent" god for these reasons is not to show all men have.

## Nietzsche

As the other men mentioned, Frederick Nietzsche often elicits strangely ambivalent feelings in the lives of many theists. I for one am deeply impressed not only by his insights but by his passion. Like Kierkegaard, Nietzsche offers a devastating critique of organized religion that I can deeply appreciate. His description of the decadence of European society, particularly at the moral level, is helpful. That heroic moral courage is all too often compromised or sacrificed to the security of the herd is axiomatic. If life is ultimately without value and man's basic characteristic is his lust for power, then Nietzsche has offered powerful reasons for negating not only God but religion as well. If the only reason people are religious is to escape the burden of dialectical courage, then I would campaign for the end of religion. But again, these matters do not touch the issue of the existence of God, though they press heavily on the matter of religious behavior.

Thus, while valuable insights may be gained with respect to human behavior by an analysis of the possible and actual role psychological desires play in religion, the question of the existence of God cannot be solved by these considerations. What is true can never be determined by an analysis of what men desire or do not desire to be the truth.

## CHAPTER 4

# The Psychology of Atheism

By now the views of Marx, Freud, Nietzsche, etc., have been so widely disseminated that it is a common occurrence for the theist to have his faith challenged on the basis of psychological charges. It would almost require the lamp of Diogenes to discover a religious man who has never been accused of believing in God merely because he needed a crutch to face the threatening contingencies of the modern world. That the shoe could be on the other foot or the crutch used for the other leg is rarely considered.

In contrast to the widespread awareness of psychology of theism, there is a woeful ignorance of a theoretical basis for a psychology of atheism. It is not common knowledge that the New Testament offers an answer to the question, "If there is a God, why is there atheism?" The answer to the question is given in what would now be called psychological categories. That is to say, the New Testament maintains that unbelief is generated not so much by intellectual causes as by moral and psychological ones. The problem is not that there is insufficient evidence to convince rational beings that there is a God, but that rational beings have a natural antipathy to the being of God. In a word, the nature of God (at least the Christian God) is *repugnant* to man and is not the focus of desire or wish-projection. Man's desire is not that Yahweh exists, but that He doesn't. The New Testament sees not only atheism but human fabricated religion as being grounded in such antipathy.

To gain a clear understanding of the charge leveled at natural man, it will be helpful to take a close look at the Apostle Paul's letter to the Romans. In the first chapter of that epistle, Paul gives an elaborate explanation of man's reaction to the knowledge of God. What follows is an analysis of his argument beginning at verse eighteen.

> For the wrath of God is revealed from heaven against all ungodliness and wickedness of men who by their wickedness suppress the truth. (Rom. 1:18)

Paul begins by declaring the revelation of the wrath of God from heaven. This initial assertion is enough in itself to provoke a negative emotional reaction by many readers. The idea of the wrath of God is not a popular concept. The word Paul uses, which is translated by the English "wrath," is the Greek word ὀργή (orge). The Latin version translates the Greek by the work *ira*. The wrath that Paul describes does not indicate an arbitrary, capricious, or irrational passion manifested in the deity. Though God is indeed angry, His anger is directed to, and provoked by, the evil of men. Paul knows nothing of a divine blind fury that rages against innocent men. God's wrath is revealed against *ungodliness* and *unrighteousness* of men.

Ungodliness is a general term capable of various forms of particular content. The term ἀσέβεια (asabea) involves a general conduct of impiety and irreligiosity. Ungodliness involves a state of opposition to the majesty of God. Unrighteousness, ἀδικία (adikia), indicates an assault against the righteousness of God. Many commentators interpret this passage as referring to two different kinds of human activity, namely, impiety and immorality. John Murray, for example, writes:

> "Ungodliness" refers to perversity that is religious in character, "unrighteousness" to what is moral; the former is illustrated by idolatry, the latter by immorality. The order is, no doubt, significant. In the apostle's description of the degeneracy, impiety is the precursor of immorality.[1]

Contrary to Murray, I adopt the position taken by Calvin and more recently by Kittel:

> A common view is that the reference is to sins against the first and second tables of the Law, offences against God and neighbor. If so, it is natural to conclude, though there is no exegetical support for this, that Paul has irreligion and immorality in view, and that the former is traced back to the latter. Against this, however, is the πᾶσαν which embraces both terms and binds them closely together. Another counterargument is that the distinction between sins against God and against men is rare among the Rabbis and is certainly not a Rabbinic distinction. A final point is that in what follows ἀδικία covers both words. The δίκη against which men offend is God's righteousness. Hence ασέβεια and ἀδικία in R. 1:18 are a hendiadys: "ungodliness and unrighteousness."[2]

Thus the same general idea is expressed by the use of two different nouns. God's wrath is directed against something specific which is considered to be an expression of both ungodliness and unrighteousness.

Paul does not leave us to speculate as to the particular evil men commit that is considered ungodly and unrighteous. He moves quickly from the general to the specific and locates the particular crime that provokes God. That crime is identified as wickedness that *suppresses the truth*. It is this suppression of the truth that is at the heart of Paul's psychology of atheism. Paul uses the expression ἐν ἀδικίᾳ κατεχόντων, which has been variously translated, "holding (the truth) in unrighteousness," hold down (the truth) in unrighteousness, hinder (the truth)..., in wickedness stifling the truth..., etc. Thus the word κατεχόντων, is variously translated "hold," "hold down," "suppress," "stifle," and "hinder." J. H. Bavinck has suggested another alternative to get at the matter, namely the word "repress." He writes:

> It seems to me that in this case we should translate it by "repress." We intentionally choose a word which has a specific meaning in psychological literature. Webster's *New Collegiate Dictionary* defines the word "repression" as "the process by which unacceptable desires or impulses are excluded from consciousness and thus being denied direct satisfaction are left to operate in the unconscious." This seems to agree with what Paul says here about human life. But we must mention that the word *repression* has received a wider meaning in more recent psychology. In Freudian psychology it specifically refers to unconscious desires of a more or less sexual nature. In more recent psychology it is also applied to desires and impulses of a very different nature. The impulses or desires which are repressed may be very valuable. Anything that goes contrary to the accepted patterns of life or to the predominant popular ideas may be repressed. Usually this happens and the results can be far-reaching. We are reminded of this psychological phenomenon recently

discovered by Paul's usage of this word. He says that man always naturally represses God's truth because it is contrary to his pattern of life.[3]

The primary meaning of the verb κατέχειν in Biblical Greek is "to hold fast." In its most common usage it is a positive term such as "holding fast" to spiritual values, the word of God, etc. But the term is also used in a pejorative sense meaning "holding illegally" or "holding in prison."[4] Paul, in Romans 1, is obviously using the term in a negative sense. Thus, man is said to *hold* the truth in an evil way. According to Bavinck it is a repressing or "holding down" of truth that ought not to be repressed or held down.

> For what can be known about God is plain to them, because God has shown it to them. (Rom. 1:19)

Here the Apostle asserts that knowledge of God is not a problem of obscurity that can be detected only by a gnostic elite group or by a skilled master of esoteric mysteries. That which can be known is plain. The word "plain" is rendered in the Greek by φανερόν (phaneron) and in the Latin by *manifestum*. This knowledge (γνωστόν) is not hidden or concealed, but manifest. It is clear and transparent for anyone to see. Paul goes on to say that the reason it is *plain* is because God shows it to them. In this case if the pupil doesn't learn, it is not because the teacher didn't teach. Not only is the knowledge plainly available but the knowledge is made clear by God himself.

> Ever since the creation of the world his invisible nature, namely, his eternal power and deity, has been clearly perceived in the things that have been made. So that they are without excuse. (Rom. 1:20)

Much debate has arisen in the history of the church concerning the precise meaning of this verse.

The debate centers around the controversy over whether God's revelation is *mediate* or *immediate.* That is, is the revelation gleaned (by reasoning) from the evidence of God in the creation or is the revelation a kind of *apriori* knowledge immediately impressed upon the consciousness of man? [5] The question arises from a certain ambiguity in the Greek text. What does Paul mean when he says, "from the creation of the world"? Does this "from" (ἀπό) mean a temporal period or a modal source of information? Most modern commentators favor the former and render the Greek, "since" the creation of the world. Either translation is useful, however, for the point under consideration. Whatever the mode of revelation, the fact remains that God's invisible nature, even His power and deity, has been clearly perceived in the things that are made. Murray says:

> And this sense of the term "clearly seen" is provided by the explanatory clause "being understood by the things that are made"—it is the seeing of understanding of intelligent conception. Stress is laid upon the perspicuity afforded by the things that are made in mediating to us the perception of the invisible attributes—they are "clearly seen." [6]

The things that are clearly seen are seen in the created things, namely nature. The cumulative effect of this knowledge which is clearly seen is to leave men "without excuse." Herein lies the basis of the universal guilt of man. No one can claim ignorance of the knowledge of God. No one can cite insufficient evidence for not believing in God. Though people are not persuaded by the evidence does not indicate an insufficiency in the evidence, but rather an insufficiency in man. This insufficiency is not a natural inability that provides man with an excuse. Man's failure to "see" this general and universal revelation of God is not because he lacks eyes or ears or a brain with which to think. The problem is not a lack of knowledge or a lack of natural cognitive equipment but is a moral deficiency. Hence man is held culpable for his refusal to submit to the evidence God plainly provides. This critical distinction between the objective data and the subjective appropriation of it is one that is overlooked far too often. If man had no natural cognitive ability to receive the general revelation, God could hardly hold him responsible for it. But no such excuse can be claimed by man as Paul emphatically states. Calvin says on this point:

> But as the greater part of mankind, enslaved by error, walk blindfold in this glorious theater, he exclaims that it is a rare and singular wisdom to meditate carefully on these works of God, which many, who seem most sharp-sighted in other respects, behold without profit. It is indeed true, that the brightest manifestation of divine glory finds not one genuine spectator among a hundred. Still neither his power nor his wisdom is shrouded in darkness.[7]

To be sure, Calvin declares a kind of insufficiency of general revelation. It is insufficient to "lead us to the right path." That is, as Calvin elaborates, it is insufficient to convert us. He also speaks of a deficiency of the "natural powers" of man, but is careful to point out that "as the dullness which prevents us is within, there is no room for excuse. We cannot plead ignorance, without being at the same time convicted by our own consciences both of sloth and ingratitude."[8] Elsewhere he comments, "We must, therefore, make this distinction, that the manifestation of God by which He makes His glory known among His creatures is sufficiently clear as far as its own light is concerned."[9]

Thus the lack of deficiency in general revelation is rooted not so much in man's natural composition as in his disposition. That is, the matter of the knowledge of God the Creator is not so much an intellectual problem as it is a moral problem. It becomes an intellectual problem because the mind is darkened by man's indisposition or psychological bias against the light. As Jesus indicated, "Light came into the world, but men loved the darkness rather than the light because their deeds were evil" (John 3:19).

> For although they knew God they did not honor him as God or give thanks to him, but they became futile in their thinking and their senseless minds were darkened. (Rom. 1:21)

Again Paul reaffirms that men "knew" God. The problem is not failure to honor what was not known, but a refusal to honor what was clearly known.

Paul not only asserts that revelation is provided and made available but asserts that the revelation penetrates man. Here I must fault Calvin for his use of the "blindfold image." It is not as though God merely provides light and men refuse to look at it. The light gets through (as Calvin himself indicates). We not only have an external revelation but we have a knowledge of that revelation. To argue that general revelation fails to produce a "natural knowledge" of God is to do serious violence to the text. Paul's complaint is not that men failed to know God, but that they failed to honor Him. Herein is the universal indictment of man.

Again, it is critical to repeat that the indictment is not rendered against men who are ignorant with or without just cause. There can be no appeal to invincible or vincible ignorance of the knowledge of God. If there were no universal general revelation, an appeal could be lodged against God that His wrath was being directed not only against people who knew nothing about Him, but against people who had no possible way of knowing anything about Him. That would be to hold people accountable for ignorance that was invincible (unable to be overcome). But the point is that such a revelation is given so that invincible ignorance cannot be the plea.

But what about vincible ignorance, ignorance that results from a refusal to make use of the data made available to you? Can the atheist plead that although the revelation was made available and manifested clearly, objectively, and transparently, he didn't "see" it because in his fear or pride or antipathy of any sort, he refused to open his eyes to it? The answer must again be in the negative as Paul makes it clear that the light penetrates—knowledge is there. The judgment is not leveled in terms of ignorance, vincible or invincible, but against the "holding of the truth" in unrighteousness. Knowledgeable men, not ignorant men, are the focal points of divine wrath and judgment.

In the use of the term "knowledge of God" in the New Testament, there are clear indications that this ($\gamma\nu\hat{\omega}\sigma\iota\varsigma$) or knowledge can be on different levels. The term is a pregnant one, filled with various nuances. There is a difference between "knowing" God theoretically and knowing Him personally, in terms of an intimate filial relationship. There is also the crucial difference between a knowledge of God and an acknowledgement of God which is precisely what the Apostle is dealing with here.[10] *Men are judged for refusing to acknowledge what they know to be true.* No matter how many nuances or levels may be contained in the word $\gamma\nu\hat{\omega}\sigma\iota\varsigma$ (knowledge), there remains the decisive distinction between $\gnosis$ (knowledge) and[I] $\agnosia$ (ignorance).

The Apostle goes on to say that men who failed to honor God or give thanks to Him (even while knowing Him) became futile in their thinking and their senseless hearts were darkened. What follows from the refusal to acknowledge God is the effect of futile reasoning. This reasoning is futile precisely because it proceeds from a primary premise that is faulty and produces only the final fruit already present in the initial bias. The end result is not light, but darkness, that penetrates to the very heart or core of man. It ends in darkness because it abhors the light at the beginning. Had the reason first acknowledged the clear presence of the light, the fatal process of reasoning would have never begun. Brilliant and erudite reasoning may produce abhorrent conclusions if they proceed from a faulty starting point. A scientist who refuses to acknowledge facts that he knows are true can hardly be expected to arrive at sound conclusions. Any reasoning process that begins with a denial of the known and proceeds on the basis of prejudice can hardly produce light, no matter how lucid and cogent the argument may proceed after the initial error is made.

It is important to note at this point that Paul does not deny the ability of natural man to reason or even to reason correctly if free of prejudice. Again, the problem is not in the capacity for thought *per se*, but is located in the problem of a thought process that begins and is maintained by prejudice to the facts. The intellectual problem is produced by the moral problem, not the moral problem by an intellectual one.

> Claiming to be wise, they became fools, and exchanged the glory of the immortal God for images

resembling mortal man or birds or animals or reptiles. (Rom. 1:22, 23)

This severe indictment by the Apostle could easily be misconstrued as an assault upon the intelligence of natural man. A close look, however, of this passage, will indicate that this passage again attacks not the intellectual ability of men but their morality. Paul's use of the term "fools" must be examined closely.

In Biblical categories the term "fool" does not necessarily indicate a person of low intelligence. The term connotes both a moral and religious judgment. To be sure, the word is capable of being used to describe persons who are dull-witted or have an extraordinarily low degree of common sense. The term μωρός (moros) is the root from which the English word "moron" derives. In classical Greek the term had a psychological flavor. Bertram points out:

> With reference to men the use is predominantly psychological. The word implies censure on man himself: his acts, thoughts, counsels, and words are not as they should be. The weakness may be due to a specific failure in judgment or decision, but a general deficiency of intellectual and spiritual capacities may also be asserted.[11]

In Old Testament terms the fool stands in sharp contrast to the wise man. The wise man is known not by his academic credentials but by his practical manifestation of godliness. Wisdom begins with the "fear of the Lord." Conversely, foolishness has its origin in the rejection of God. It is the "fool" who says in his heart there is no God (Ps. 14:1). Isaiah calls the man a fool who contemptuously breaks off fellowship with God and becomes a practical atheist. To be a fool is to fall into a negative theological category rather than an exclusively intellectual one. Likewise the "fool" of the New Testament is the one who fails to act prudently with respect to God, falling under moral judgment.

Paul's critique in this text is a two-edged sword. Not only is the natural man labeled a fool but is pronounced guilty of hypocrisy as well. The one who becomes a fool is the same one who professes to be wise. There is a serious discrepancy between a profession of wisdom and the reality of wisdom. The man's guilt is compounded by the fact that while being a fool he proclaims that he is wise. He claims a state he doesn't have and thus falls under the double indictment of the Apostle.

The foolishness of man in manifested in the exchanging of the glory of God for idols. The word "exchange" is important to a proper understanding of the text. Many translations often render the verb to mean simply "change." But the total context of the passage excludes this rendition as it is too weak and ambiguous. A particular kind of change is in view here; one that involves a mutation (see the Latin *mutauerunt*) or a distortion that involves a kind of substitution of one thing for another. This substitution involves the replacing of the genuine with the artificial or the counterfeit. (The physiological ramifications of this "exchange" will be explored later.) The change results in idolatry which also comes under the judgment of God. Here is an example of a case where the distortion of truth results not in militant atheism but in a kind of religion. This religion, however, does not serve to exonerate man or mitigate the wrath of God, but rather compounds the felony as it adds massive insult to the glory of the immortal God. Here pagan religion is not viewed as a step of evolutionary progress on the way to a fully developed monotheism, but a step on the pathway of flight and retreat from monotheism. Not evolution but devolution or even revolution (in the sense of revolt against God) is the pattern of pagan religion. Murray adds:

> Here the apostle sets forth the origin of that degeneration and degradation which pagan idolatry epitomizes, and we have the biblical philosophy of false religion. "For heathenism," as Meyer says, "is not the primeval religion, from which man might gradually have risen to the knowledge of the true God, but is, on the contrary, the result of a falling away from the known original revelation of the true God in His works." [12]

Mircea Eliade writes about the notion of a "remote God" that is found widely in primitive religions. He says:

> Celestially structured supreme beings tend to disappear from the practice of religion, from cult; they depart from among men, withdraw to the sky, and become remote, inactive gods (*dei otiosi*). In short, it may be said of these gods that, after creating the cosmos, life, and man, they feel a sort of fatigue, as if the immense enterprise of the creation had exhausted their resources. So they withdraw to the sky, leaving a son or a demiurge on earth to finish or perfect the Creation. Gradually their place is taken by other divine figures—the mythical ancestors, the mother-goddesses, the fecundating gods, and the like.[13]

Eliade goes on to say that among African peoples, "The great celestial god, the supreme being, all-powerful creator, plays only a minor role in the religious life of most tribes. He is too far away or too good to need an actual cult, and he is involved only in extreme cases." [14]

Thus, even in primitive religion there is at least a vague recollection of God the Creator that remains remote. According to Paul, religion is not the fruit of a zealous pursuit of God, but the result of a passionate flight from God. The glory of God is exchanged for an idol. The idol stands as a monument not to religious fervor but to the flight of man from his initial encounter with the glory of God.

> Therefore God gave them up in the lusts of their hearts to impurity, to the dishonoring of their bodies among themselves, because they exchanged the truth about God for a lie and worshipped and served the creature rather than the Creator, who is blessed forever! Amen. (Rom. 1:24, 25)

The response of God to the work of idolatry is seen in a kind of divine abandonment of men. God lets the man pursue his lusts or desires for impurity. The working out of this abandoned lust culminates in the dishonoring of the human. What begins as an act of refusal to honor God ends in the dishonoring of men. Karl Barth comments:

> When God has been deprived of His glory, men are also deprived of theirs. Desecrated within their souls, they are desecrated also without in their bodies, for men are one.[15]

Paul's analysis indicates a progression not only from God to man but also from thought to deed. As behavior and theory are distinguishable, yet inseparably related, the moral consequences of the rejection of the knowledge of God will be inevitably manifested in moral conduct. Luther adds:

> Hence, also, the guilt is greater, for the aberration of idolatry and of an empty knowledge of God is now sealed not merely in the mind but in deed and action, thus becoming an example and a stumbling

block that leads others into temptation. When, within the limits of their reverence for his holy name, they disgrace God in their thoughts by conceiving of him in a fashion that is more than unworthy of him, it is only right that they should fall back upon their heads, and that they should think and correspondingly act in a way that is unworthy of their humanity.[16]

Paul again makes reference to an "exchange" that is involved in idolatry. The exchange involves the substitution of a lie in place of the truth of God. This is the essence of idolatry, namely the worshipping of the created realm in place of, or instead of, the Creator. In the practice of idolatrous religion the intrinsic antithesis between truth and falsehood is obscured.[17] That the pagan is "religious" in no way mollifies his guilt before God. Again, the practice of idolatrous religion is not viewed as an approximate form of authentic religion but rests on the negation of it. It is one thing to deny the existence of God; it is another thing to add insult to the denial by worshipping as God something that is clearly of the created order. The worship and service rendered to idols may be sincere—yet it is regarded as being sincerely evil. A "sincere" distortion of the truth that dishonors God evokes nothing less than the sincere wrath of God. As Paul elsewhere indicates in his reaction to the Greeks at Mars' Hill in Athens, God is not particularly pleased or flattered by altars inscribed with the legend, "TO THE UNKNOWN GOD." Such worship is declared as being grounded in superstition rather than reality.

> For this reason God gave them up to dishonorable passions. Their women exchanged natural relations for unnatural, and men likewise gave up natural relations with women and were consumed with pas-

sion for one another, men committing shameless acts with men and receiving in their own persons the due penalty for their error. (Rom. 1:26, 27)

Again the Apostle speaks of God's "giving them up." God removes the restraints from those who flee from Him and allows them to follow the course of their own drives. Their dishonorable degeneracy is in no way limited to homosexual practices, but is made particularly manifest by that activity. It is not strange that Paul should appeal to homosexuality as an indication of radical degeneracy in light of the Old Testament view of it. Under the Mosaic Law homosexuality was regarded as an abomination to God and was a capital crime. It was also viewed as a serious enough sin to defile the land and a type of sin that was considered part of the customary practices of pagan nations with which Israel was forbidden to consort.[18]

And since they did not see fit to acknowledge God, God gave them up to a base mind and to improper conduct. (Rom. 1:28)

Again Paul approaches his theme in another way. The giving up to a base mind and improper conduct is not an arbitrary action of God. There is a reason for this punitive measure. The reason is clear: "they did not see fit to acknowledge God." The judgment of man upon God was the judgment that God was not worthy of human consideration. Again the error of the human mind does not proceed from a mere logical miscalculation. It was not an error flowing out of syllogistic reasoning but a deliberate evaluation of the worth of the knowledge of God. The error of the pagan is not fortuitous, but clearly deliberate. The "not seeing fit" is an obstinate refusal to acknowledge that which is manifestly true.

> They were filled with all manner of wickedness, evil, covetousness, malice. Full of envy, murder, strife, deceit, malignity, they are gossips, slanderers, haters of God, insolent, haughty, boastful, inventors of evil, disobedient to parents, foolish, faithless, heartless, ruthless. Though they know God's decree that those who do such things deserve to die, they not only do them but approve those who practice them. (Rom. 1:29-32)

This catalogue of crimes arising out of an initial rejection of the knowledge of God is at best, ghastly. This grisly list of human violations of divine law does not indicate that man's problem of psychological prejudice toward God is a mild one. Indeed, the hostility is deep and reflects not a minor disinclination, but a burning rage in the very heart of man.

Another element is added to the content of the knowledge of God revealed in creation. Not only is God's existence known, but His attitude toward evil is likewise made manifest.[19] The pagan knows the penalty for his evil. The astonishing dimension of the pagan's madness, however, is seen not only in that he blatantly practices what he knows to be evil, and knows will be punished, but he applauds and encourages others to participate in his madness with him. Murray remarks:

> To put it bluntly, we are not only bent on damning ourselves but we congratulate others in the doing of those things that we know have their issue in damnation. We hate others as we hate ourselves and render therefore to them the approval of what we know merits damnation. Iniquity is most aggravated when it meets with no inhibition from the disapproval of others and when there is collective, undissenting approbation.[20]

The foregoing conclusion with respect to the immoral character of human behavior sets in bold relief the utter folly of it. This description of human endeavor manifests a kind of mass insanity. Insane not in the sense of behavior that is radically abnormal or atypical, but rather a kind of "normal" madness which is the inevitable result of an irrational process. Sin in the lives of rational beings begins on an irrational foundation: the refusal to acknowledge as true what one knows with clarity to be true.

The list of evils Paul enumerates are not to be found exclusively in the confines of special isolated groups of a particularly degenerate or primitive society. Paul is not describing the savage behavior of some remote tribe of head-hunting cannibals or the moral pattern of the most calloused men in a maximum security prison. How many lamps would Diogenes need to find a man free from covetousness? Where could he go in his pursuit for a man without envy? What society includes human beings free from insolence, boastfulness, and haughtiness? No, the evils elucidated are "normal" and "typical" of man qua man. They are manifestations of the normal *irrationalism* of the most sophisticated society. Why? Why does rational man behave in such an irrational manner? Can we explain this by appealing to a subliminal sex drive. Have we answered the question adequately by simply appealing to Nietzsche's "lust for power"? From whence cometh this "lust for power"?

## The Psychology of Romans I

To translate Paul's analysis of man's response to the knowledge of God into contemporary categories of psychology is not a difficult task, as indicated earlier by Bavinck's analysis. The basic stages of man's reaction to God can be formulated by means of the categories of *trauma, repression*, and *substitution*.

## Trauma

The term "trauma" may be defined as "an injury, wound, shock, or the resulting condition." [21] This notion of injury or shock can apply to mental, emotional, and psychological shock as well as physical. A traumatic experience generally involves something negative or threatening to the individual. (Though it is also recognized that a positive surprise can be shocking in a traumatic way.) In the case of Paul's analysis the trauma is produced by man's encounter with God's self-revelation. Confrontation with God shocks and injures man. For various reasons, which will be explored in depth in later chapters, God's presence is severely threatening to man. God manifests a threat to man's moral standards, a threat to his quest for autonomy, and a threat to his desire for concealment. God's revelation involves the intrusion and indeed invasion of the "other," the "different," the alien and strange to human circumstances. In a word, it represents the invasion of light into the darkness to which men are accustomed.

On a physical plane we are aware of the painful results produced when we emerge from a situation of prolonged darkness into the blazing brightness of sunlight. Coal miners must be careful to adjust their eyes gradually as they emerge from their subterranean labors into daylight. Even those who walk above ground in the midst of daylight must be careful not to gaze directly into the sun lest they cause traumatic damage to their eyes. Calvin notes:

> If, at mid-day, we either look down to the ground, or on surrounding objects which lie open to our

view, we think ourselves endued with a very strong and piercing eyesight; but when we look up to the sun, and gaze at it unveiled, the sight which did excellently well for the earth, is instantly so dazzled and confounded by the refulgence, as to oblige us to confess that our acuteness in discerning terrestrial objects is mere dimness when applied to the sun. Thus, too, it happens in estimating our spiritual qualities. So long as we do not look beyond the earth, we are quite pleased with our own righteousness, wisdom, and virtue; we address ourselves in the most flattering terms, and seem only less than demigods. But should we once begin to raise our thoughts to God, and reflect what kind of Being he is, and how absolute the perfection of that righteousness, and wisdom, and virtue, to which, as a standard, we are bound to be conformed, what formerly delighted us by its false show of righteousness, will become polluted with the greatest iniquity; what strangely imposed upon us under the name of wisdom, will disgust by its extreme folly; and what presented the appearance of virtuous energy, will be condemned as the most miserable impotence. So far are those qualities in us, which seem most perfect, from corresponding to the divine purity.[22]

Thus, encounter with the light of God's revelation is a traumatic experience for man. There is no trauma if the eyes are forever closed so that no light penetrates. But the eyes close in reaction to the shock of the light—after the pain has been experienced.

## *Repression*

Repression may be defined as follows: To check by or as by pressure; to restrain. To prevent the natural or normal expression, activity, or development of. In psychological terms, repression may be defined as the process by which unacceptable desires or impulses are excluded from consciousness and thus being denied direct satisfaction are left to operate in the unconscious.[23]

In the case of God's revelation, man encounters something ominously threatening which is traumatic. The memory of conscious knowledge of the trauma is not maintained in its lucid threatening state but is repressed. It is "put down" or "held in captivity" in the unconsciousness. That which is repressed is not destroyed. The memory remains though it may be buried in the subconscious realm. Knowledge of God is unacceptable to man and as a result man does his best to blot it out or at least camouflage it in such a way that its threatening character can be concealed or dulled. That the human psyche is capable of such repression has been thoroughly demonstrated in a multitude of ways. The critical factor, however, for our discussion, is that the knowledge is not obliterated or destroyed. It remains intact though deeply submerged in the unconscious.

## *Substitution*

It is because repressed knowledge is not destroyed that substitution or "exchange" (metallaso) takes place. Again Bavinck comments:

> This phenomenon of replacing, of substituting, is so common that we see it everywhere. It has been discovered that these repressed impulses of which we spoke, which "are left to operate in the unconscious," are not dead. They remain strong, and try to reassert themselves again and again. Surely, they play no part in man's conscious life, but they succeed in showing every now and again that they still exist. This has been illustrated by the story of the boy sent out of class at school who kept on

throwing stones against the windows of the school to show that he was still there. Freud particularly has called attention to this phenomenon and inaugurated its study. He noticed that the impulses which have been exiled to the unconscious may very well reveal themselves in the errors we make, in our slips of the tongue. But they especially crop up in dreams, for then they get the chance to come to the surface.[24]

In the substitution-exchange process, the repressed knowledge manifests itself outwardly in a disguised or veiled form. The original knowledge is threatening; its disguised form is much less threatening. When dealing with deep-rooted anxieties of uncertain origin, psychologists and psychiatrists frequently explore, with meticulous care, what may be termed the symbolic activity of mankind. Dreams, Freudian slips, bodily gestures, etc., all are involved in the careful scrutiny of the scientist seeking to unravel the complexities of the human psyche. For example, if in the course of a counseling interview, a person exhibits an involuntary twitch or tic every time he mentions his mother, the counselor will not deem that insignificant. He will proceed to probe further into the area of the person's past relationship with his mother, even though the person may protest profusely and give every conscious assurance that there are no problems in that area of his life. In a word, what cannot be squarely and comfortably faced in the conscious mind, may be borne with a relative degree of comfort at the unconscious level. In theological terms, what results from the repression is the profession of atheism either in militant terms, or its less militant form of agnosticism, or a kind of religion that makes God less of a threat than He really is. Either option, atheism or religion, manifests an exchange of the truth for a lie. The truth is exchanged for the lie simply because the lie seems easier to live with.

It is an interesting phenomenon to examine how people react to the Biblical notion of hell. Frequently the question is asked, "Do we take what the Bible says about hell literally or is it just symbolism?" The Biblical images of hell are indeed frightening. Such images as a "lake of fire where the worm doesn't die," or the "pit of everlasting darkness," etc., are horrible notions to contemplate. Most people breathe an audible sigh of relief when I respond to the question of literalism versus symbolism in favor of symbolism. They are relieved to think that such graphic images are "just symbols." Symbols we can live with—it's the reality toward which the symbols point that is often so repugnant to us. I have found, incidentally, that the sigh of relief expressed when I allow that the Biblical images of hell are symbols, is quickly supplanted by a gasp of horror when I raise the question that must be faced with respect to the Biblical imagery of hell: "Why did Jesus use such terrifying symbols to describe hell?" If the symbols are terrifying, what does that suggest about the reality toward which they point? Many people do not particularly enjoy contemplating that, but would prefer to halt the discussion at the point of "just symbols."

The judgment of the New Testament is that religion is, in many cases, man-made. Karl Barth pointed out that even Christianity can and often does become such a religion. This "religion" expresses not the fruit of man's pursuit of God, but the product of his substitution-exchange propensity. Bavinck goes on to say with respect to religion:

> Thus, all kinds of ideas of God are formed; the human mind as the *fabrica idolorum* (Calvin) makes

its own ideas of God and its own myths. This is not intentional deceit—it happens without man's knowing it. He cannot get rid of them. So he has religion; he is busy with a god; he serves his god—but he does not see that the god he serves is not God Himself. An exchange has taken place—a perilous exchange. An essential quality of God has been blurred because it did not fit in with the human pattern of life, and the image man has of God is no longer true. Divine revelation indeed lies at the root of it, but man's thoughts and aspirations cannot receive it and adapt themselves to it. In the image man has of God we can recognize the image of man himself.[25]

The idea that man is capable of and has a proclivity for the manufacture of religion is not unique with Freud, Feuerback, or Marx. Calvin pointed that out in the sixteenth century appealing to sources originating centuries earlier. That human religion reveals much of man's desires is clearly obvious. But it must be insisted that at least the Biblical God manifests characteristics and features that are less than desirable for most men. With the numerous references to His expressions of wrath and judgment, His absolute claim over human life, etc., is it any surprise that His appearance is traumatic?

The Christian church has had to struggle in every generation against those who would mollify the threatening dimension of God by substitution and distortion. The twentieth century is no exception. We have witnessed massive attempts to soften the demands imposed upon us by the Biblical God. Consider, for example, the Bultmannian school which seeks to demythologize the Scriptures and produces a theology ripped out of the threatening character of history. An analysis of this anti-historical and anti-intellectual approach to theology inevitably raises the question as to the actual locus of mythology. Is it in the New Testament or in the reconstructed Christianity the school represents? It is equally interesting to see the end result of Paul Tillich's God-beyond-God of "ultimate concern." In spite of Tillich's literal apoplexy over the claims of his followers, he was the motivating force behind the proclamation of the death-of-God and the rise of "Christian atheism." A strange irony attaches itself to much of contemporary theology. The "hard sayings" of Jesus are removed from the danger zone of encounter, the motifs of transcendance and "otherness" are rendered safe by demythologizing and Jesus is reduced to the realm of the "conditioned." Gollwitzer raises the obvious question, "Why should anyone attach unconditional importance to that which is conditioned?" [26] That question sounds strangely like the kind of question the prophets of Israel raised to those who fashioned idols out of wood and stone and then proceeded to bow down and worship the work of their own hands.

## CHAPTER 5

# The Trauma of Holiness

In 1910 a book was published in Germany under the simple title, *Das Heilige* (The Holy). In this short work Rudolf Otto paved the way for a new evaluation of religious experience. Otto's work, which appeared under the English title *The Idea of the Holy*, was virtually unique in its peculiar approach. Instead of examining the ideas found in various religions of the world, Otto studied the phenomenon of human reaction to the experience of the holy. Mircea Eliade says of Otto:

> Gifted with great psychological subtlety, and thoroughly prepared by his two-fold training as theologian and historian of religions, he succeeded in determining the content and specific characteristics of religious experience. Passing over the rational and speculative side of religion, he concentrated chiefly on its irrational aspect.[1]

Though Otto sought to explore and analyze the "irrational" or "non-rational" dimension of religion from a phenomenological perspective, he was in no way seeking to instruct or enhance an irrationalism or subjectivism in theology. He says in the foreword of the English edition:

I do not thereby want to promote in any way the tendency of our time towards an extravagant and fantastic 'irrationalism,' but rather to join issue with it in its morbid form. The 'irrational' is today a favorite theme of all who are too lazy to think or too ready to evade the arduous duty of clarifying their ideas and grounding their convictions on a basis of coherent thought.[2]

In his analysis of the word "holy" Otto points out that, though the moral quality of goodness is present in the term, it cannot be exhausted by it or equated with it. Though the holy contains the notion of absolute goodness, there remains a certain "extra," an "overplus." Thus "overplus" is defined by Otto as the "numinous." He says:

> I shall speak, then, of a unique 'numinous' category of value and of a definitely 'numinous' state of mind, which is always found wherever the category is applied. This mental state is perfectly *sui generis* and irreducible to any other; and therefore, like every absolutely primary and elementary datum, while it admits of being discussed, it cannot be strictly defined.[3]

The experience of the numinous provides what Otto calls "creature-feeling." [4] This feeling involves a band of feeling of dependence that is "a first subjective concomitant and effect of another feeling —element, which casts it like a shadow, but which in itself indubitably has immediate and primary reference to an object outside the self." [5] That is, in the experience of the numinous the resultant feeling of creatureliness is a subjective response to the objective numinous.

The feeling of terror is basic to the experience of the holy and sacred. In further analysis Otto adopts the term *mysterium tremendum* to capture the experience of the Holy.

## Mysterium Tremendum

Otto analyzes the notion of tremendum by isolating its constituent elements. First is the element of awefulness. This awefulness is of a peculiar nature. The emotion of fear is closely connected with it, but again not directly equated. We derive words like *tremor* or *tremble* from the concept of tremendum. The fear associated with the element of *awefulness* is one that produces *tremors* or trembling. We think of Kierkegaard's panegyric upon Abraham in his *Fear and Trembling* in which he scrutinizes the peculiar kind of 'aweful dread that is experienced in the presence of God.' Or we think of the negro spiritual, *Were You There When They Crucified My Lord?* with its ominous refrain, "Sometimes it causes me to tremble . . . tremble . . . tremble."

Otto notes the close relationship between the awefulness element and the Greek term σεβαστός. This title in its Latin form is *augustus*. He notes the early Christian antipathy to the use of the title *augustus* with reference to any man, even the emperor. "They felt that to call a man σεβαστός was to give a human being a name proper only the the *numen*, to rank him by the category proper only to the *numen*, and that it therefore amounted to a kind of idolatry." [6]

This kind of feeling is aweful not in the sense of being bad but in a literal sense of being "full of awe." This awe is a kind of reverential fear that produces a shuddering kind of dread. The development of the usage of the term awful suggests that there is a strong negative feeling associated with the experience of religious awe. The term awful is now used almost as a synonym for bad or very bad.

The second element of the tremendum is the element of *"overpoweringness."* Otto links this awareness of might and power with the Latin *majestas*. Confrontation with this majestic power evokes a sense of impotence and general nothingness. A Biblical example of this dimension of encounter with the Holy may be seen in the case of Job.

After the narrative relating Job's experience with miserable afflictions, softened not at all by the judgmental counsel of his friends, nor the shrewish scorn of his wife, we read of Job's plea for an answer to his condition from God:

> Oh that I had one to hear me! Behold, here is my signiture; let the Almighty answer me! And the indictment which my adversary has written....
> (Job 31:35)

In this plea Job addresses God as the "Almighty." The particular title he uses is the term *El Shaddai*. This name for God appears more frequenly in the book of Job (30 times) than in any other book of the Old Testament. The name dates from Patriarchal times and connotes strongly the awesome power of God. Various renditions of El Shaddai include "the Destroyer," "the All-Powerful One" and "the Overpowerer." [7]

Following the discourse of Elihu, God responds to Job in terms of an overpowering interrogation. God begins the interrogation with a devastating question that at the same time pronounces a judgment on Job:

> "Who is this that darkens counsel by words without knowledge? Now gird up your loins like a man, and I will ask you, and you instruct Me!" (Job 38:2, 3)

What follows is a lengthy series of questions that leave Job in a state of near collapse. Such questions as:

> "Where were you when I laid the foundations of the earth? Who laid its cornerstone...? Have the gates of death been revealed to you...? Can you bind the chains of the Pleiades; or loose the cords of Orion?... Do you know the time the mountain goats give birth? Do you observe the calving of the deer?... Is it by your understanding that the hawk soars, stretching his wings toward the south?" (Job 38, 39)

And so the interrogation proceeds until God brings it to a halt by a direct question of Job:

> "Will the faultfinder contend with the Almighty? Let him who reproves God answer it." (Job 40:1, 2)

Notice Job's reaction. He cries out:

> "Behold, I am insignificant; what can I reply to Thee? I lay my hand on my mouth. Once I have spoken, and I will not answer; even twice, and I will add no more." (Job 40:3-5)

Job's reaction manifests a classic response of a sense of insignificance and impotence when confronted by the "overpoweringness" of the Holy.

A similar episode indicated by the Prophet Jeremiah manifests the same kind of human response to the "overpoweringness" of God. He cries out to God:

> "O Lord, Thou hast deceived me and I was deceived; Thou hast overcome me and prevailed...." (Jer. 20:7)

Here Jeremiah experiences being "overwhelmed" by God. Again Eliade says:

> He finds *the feeling of terror* before the sacred, before the awe-inspiring mystery (*Mysterium tremendum*), the majesty (*majestas*) that emanates an overwhelming superiority of power....[8]

There is a sense in which confrontation with absolute power produces a sense of absolute intimidation.

The third element of the tremendum isolated by Otto is the element of "energy" or urgency. This has to do with the features of the numinous object. Otto says:

> It is particularly vividly perceptible in the ὀργή or 'wrath'; and it everywhere clothes itself in symbolical expressions—vitality, passion, emotional temper, will, force, movement, excitement, activity, impetus.[9]

In the human experience of the Holy, the Holy is not encountered in a torpid state. The Holy is not experienced as "Being-in-Inertia" or as a neutral idea. There is something dynamic and moving in the encounter. This dynamic element, whether it be wrath or love, is in part responsible for the human reaction. The reaction is not to a *static* reality, but to an active one. Thus the Holy is encountered not as a sleeping giant who can be safely avoided by careful circumnavigation but as one whose dynamism is overwelming.

### The Mysterium

That mankind finds something "mysterious" about the Holy is not surprising. In the age of radio in the '40s one of the most popular mystery programs was called "Inner Sanctum." Part of the suspenseful intrigue of the program was focused on its opening theme; the eerie, spine-tingling sound of a door creaking open as the announcer ominously said, "Inner Sanctum...." Notice that the name of the program was not inner *mysterium* but inner sanctum. Literally the name of the program was "in the holy." Even in this popular mode of communication a link was seen between the holy and the mysterious.

According to Otto, the *mysterium* is closely linked to the "Otherness" of the Holy. The strangeness and unknown dimension of the Holy adds to the spirit of fear that attends encounter with it. Though terrifying, the "Other" is also in a certain sense fascinating. There is the strange admixture of daunting awefulness with something uniquely attractive and fascinating. Otto says:

> These two qualities, the daunting and the fascinating, now combine in a strange harmony of contrasts, and the resultant dual character of the numinous consciousness, to the which entire religious development bears witness, at any rate from the level of the 'daemonic dread' onwards, is at once the strangest and most noteworthy phenomenon in in the whole history of religion. The daemonic-divine object may appear to the mind, an object of horror and dread, but at the same time it is no less something that allures with a potent charm, and the creature, who trembles before it, utterly cowed and cast down, has always at the same time the impulse to turn to it, nay, even to make it somehow his own.[10]

A child's fascination with ghost stories is a typical manifestation of the peculiar combination of fear and fascination. Children beg to hear such tales and yet often fail to endure the telling of them. My own seven-year-old son begged me last summer for permission to sleep out in the forest on a nearby mountain with a visiting college student. He thought it would be a spooky experience that would also be fun. The adventure began with unspeakable daring-do and gusto. However, after the campfire died and the conversation in the tent ceased, my junior-explorer was left in the darkness with his attention riveted to those things that "go bump in the night." He said nothing for thirty minutes but finally turned to the college student and said, "Joe, you know, there are a lot of things I don't like about this!" Joe was astute enough to interpret this casual comment and they both showed up at the back door about 1:00 a.m.

My son comes by this fascination for the terrifying quite naturally. His mother is quite addicted to the best (or worst) Hollywood "horror movies." My wife loves to view such movies, but unfortunately she cannot abide to watch them alone. She requests my companionship during her viewing pleasure, quite to my dismay. The consummate result of such episodes is that my wife is left in a state of veritable horror, and I emerge brutally bruised by her hysterical clutching and grasping of me in her fear.

Thus we are fearful, yet fascinated by the Holy. We can approach it—yet we must somehow keep a safe distance from it. We deal with it—but only after camouflaging an appropriate proportion of its terror.

### The Threat of Disintegration

Otto's analysis has shown manifestly that the human experience with the Holy produces a wide variety of shocks. This traumatic character of the encounter can be summarized as involving a positive threat of disintegration. Man's self-image, individually and collectively, experiences a clear and present danger in the presence of the Holy. The sense of contrast immediately imposed is devastating to human security. Calvin notes this with particular reference to Biblical accounts of such encounters:

> Hence that *dread* and *amazement* with which the Scripture uniformly relates. Holy men were struck and *overwhelmed* whenever they beheld the presence of God. When we see those who previously stood *firm* and *secure quaking* with *fear* that the fear of death takes hold of them, they are in a

a manner, *swallowed up* and *annihilated*.—The inference to be drawn is this: *that men are never duly touched and impressed with a conviction of their insignificance until they have contrasted themselves with the majesty of God.*—Frequent examples of this *consternation* occur both in the Book of Judges and the Prophetical Writings so much so that it was a common expression of the people of God, 'we shall *die*, for we have seen the Lord.' Their *folly*, their *feebleness* and their *pollution* always derives its chief argument from descriptions of the Divine wisdom, virtue and purity.... Nor without God—for we see Abraham ready to acknowledge himself but *dust* and *ashes* the nearer he approaches the glory of the Lord; and Elijah unable to wait with unveiled face for his approach so *dreadful* is the sight. And what can man do—man who is but rottenness and a worm, when even the cherubim must veil their faces in very *terror*. To this undoubtedly the Prophet Isaiah refers when he says the moon shall be *confounded* and the sun ashamed when the Lord of Hosts shall reign. When he shall exhibit his refulgence and give a nearer view of it, the brightest objects will in comparison be covered with darkness.[11]

It is interesting to compare Otto's analysis of human reactions to the Holy with Calvin's descriptions of the feeling-states of the Biblical characters alluded to. The words in italics have a familiar ring in light of Otto's thesis. Calvin notes feelings of dread, amazement, a loss of a sense of firmness and security, a sense of fear (quaking), being swallowed up, annihilation, consternation, a fear of death, a sense of folly, feebleness, and pollution; a sense of worthlessness (dust and ashes); a sense of dread, terror, confoundedness and shame. These are not pleasant sensations or pleasurable feeling-states to the normal person. The masochist might delight in them, but the average man would not particularly enjoy them. If finding God involves these experiences, who would seek Him? Who wants to experience the loss of security and a sense of annihilation? Let us examine more closely some of the episodes Calvin mentions. First is the case of Habakkuk the prophet. Like Job, Habakkuk was exercised about the problem of evil and suffering. He begins his oracle with a lament of anguish.

> How long, O Lord, will I call for help, and Thou wilt not hear? I cry out to Thee, "Violence!" Yet thou dost not save. Why dost Thou make me see iniquity, and cause me to look on wickedness? Yes, destruction and violence are before me; strife exists and contention arises. Therefore, the law is ignored and justice is never upheld. For the wicked surround the righteous; therefore, justice comes out perverted. (Hab. 1:2-4)

The lament is followed by withdrawal to a watchtower to await the answer of God. When God responds and gives answer to his inquiry, Habakkuk exclaims:

> I heard and my inward parts trembled;
> At the sound my lips quivered,
> decay enters my bones, and
> in my place I tremble. (Hab. 3:16)

In encounter with God, Habakkuk becomes a man of trembling belly and quivering lips. What does it mean to experience a sense of decay or rottenness entering into one's bones?

Perhaps even more exemplary of the human experience of the sense of disintegration is found in the classic encounter of Isaiah with the majesty of God. Isaiah relates it in the following terms:

> In the year of King Uzziah's death, I saw the Lord sitting on a throne, lofty and exalted, with the train of His robe filling the temple. Seraphim stood

above Him, each having six wings; with two he covered his face, and with two he covered his feet, and with two he flew. And one called out to another and said, "Holy, Holy, Holy, is the Lord of hosts, the whole earth is full of His glory." And the foundations of the thresholds trembled at the voice of him who called out, while the temple was filling with smoke. Then I said, "Woe is me, for I am ruined! Because I am a man of unclean lips, and I live among a people of unclean lips; for my eyes have seen the King, the Lord of hosts." (Isa. 6:1-5)

Isaiah's response begins with an exclamation of woe. This "woefulness" reflects an experience of a sense of doom. In prophetic oracles, the oracle of woe involves the announcement of the awful impending judgment of God. The pronouncement of woe is not positive, but negative; it is not good news (Gospel) but bad news (judgment). As the Old Testament prophets use the "woe-formula" to preface the divine indictment on Israel, so Jesus uses it to preface His scathing judgment on the Pharisees of his day. "Woe unto you, scribes, and Pharisees, hyppocrites . . . ! How can you possibly escape the judgment of hell." The woe saying functions in contrast with the weal utterances of blessing as found in the beatitudes of the Sermon on the Mount. The blessing formula is benediction; the woe formula is malediction. The oracle of weal pronounces God's blessing; the oracle of woe pronounces His curse.

In the temple Isaiah's prophetic utterance is directed inwardly. He pronounces the woe of God not on the external enemies of Israel, not on the hypocrites around him; but in the presence of the majesty of God, he pronounces the malediction on himself—woe is *me*! In this pronouncement Isaiah expresses the feeling of calamity. He has been exposed to the majesty of God, and the fear of death comes upon him. He says "woe" because he feels "ruined" or "undone." Vos says of this, "This is a sense, not of general fear, but of moral dissolution." [12]

Thus in Isaiah's case, the feeling of being undone, or dissolved, or disintegrated accompanies his vision of the holiness of God. In contemporary nomenclature we use terms like "coming apart at the seams," "falling apart," "going to pieces," "being shattered," "coming unglued," "losing one's cool," etc., to describe this type of experience. To come apart is to be dis-integrated. The loss of a sense of being "integrated" or of "having it all together" produces a sense of insecurity and instability. To overcome these feeling-states men seek to be "whole." The threat of disintegration or dissolution is a serious one to man. The holiness of God manifests that threat in the superlative degree.

The disintegrating factor in Isaiah's experience is not difficult to ascertain. His self-image is destroyed as he faces himself in the light of absolute holiness. The manifestation of God's holiness functions as the supreme iconoclast. In encounter with God, Isaiah not only apprehends something about God but he also apprehends something about Isaiah. His vision of God brings with it a new vision of himself. In this experience Isaiah's ego is not simply bruised, but is smashed... and thus he feels "undone."

The self-realization that accompanies the sense of disintegration is expressed in terms of a loss of a sense of purity. He says, "For I am a man of unclean lips." This loss of cleanness or purity has an obvious moral referent. In the presence of the Holy, Isaiah feels dirty. The sense of filth, of dirt, of uncleanness is a common human feeling associated with moral guilt. When guilt feelings are resolved in the counter experience of forgiveness, men frequently use such images as being made clean or fresh or "white as snow." The feeling of being clean is a positive moral feeling; the feeling of being dirty or filthy is clearly a negative experience. Isaiah's experience would not be the focus of delight of the hedonist. It is an experience of pain, not of pleasure.

It is interesting to notice that Isaiah's apprehension of holiness did not leave him with a "holier-than-thou" attitude. His conversion was not *to* hypocrisy, but from it. Yet at the same time he did not experience his awareness of moral corruption in isolation from its corporate ramifications. When Isaiah realized that his own lips were dirty, he recognized at the same time that this condition was not unique with him. He says, "I am a man of unclean lips, *and* I dwell in the midst of a people of unclean lips." Isaiah recognized in the context of traumatic shock that a contrast existed not simply between God and Isaiah, but between God and man. Isaiah saw himself on the side of the unholy, of the impure, and of the unclean.

To be sure, God did not leave Isaiah in his state of woe. He didn't leave him in dis-integration. The account goes on to relate that God dealt with Isaiah's dirty mouth. A red-hot coal was taken from the altar of the temple and placed on Isaiah's lips. The imagery of that episode is indeed awesome. What is left unsaid is perhaps even more so. Imagine the odor of burning flesh, coupled with the sound of a red-hot coal placed against moist lips. This must have been a moment of considerable pain. Isaiah underwent purification and refinement by fire. In a word, his diseased lips were cauterized. Out of the pain, however, came healing, and Isaiah left the temple an integrated man.

The New Testament provides similar experiences

involving the disciples of Jesus. We have data relating to several experiences of fear that may be helpful to our investigation. The first involves fear in the context of the threat of natural forces. We read in Mark's narrative:

> And leaving the multitude, they took Him along with them, just as He was, in the boat; and other boats were with Him. And there arose a fierce gale of wind, and the waves were breaking over the boat so much that the boat was already filling up. And He Himself was in the stern, asleep on the cushion; and they awoke Him and said to Him, "Teacher, do You not care that we are perishing?" And being aroused, He rebuked the wind and said to the sea, "Hush, be still." And the wind died down and it became perfectly calm. And He said to them, "Why are you so timid? How is it that you have no faith?" And they became very much afraid and said to one another, "Who then is this, that even the wind and the sea obey Him?" (Mark 4:36-41)

This narrative relates an experience involving human fear before the threatening forces of nature. Here men are faced with the perils of a tempestuous storm at sea which includes the threat of annihilation. In the face of the threat of nature the men were described as being timid or simply afraid. Yet when the threat of nature was removed the fear was not. Rather than being eliminated or even merely diminished, the fear of the men was accentuated. They were timid before the sea was calm—they were "very much afraid" after the sea was calm. In a word, the awesome manifestation of the power of Jesus was more terrifying than the storm. In this case the power of the one whose power transcends the force of nature is more threatening than the power he transcends. Here the personal threatens more than the impersonal.

Freud's thesis that men are less threatened by the personal than the impersonal cannot go unchallenged as a universal axiom. It may be generally true that personal or personalized, humanized forces are less threatening to man than impersonal forces (the validity, of course, resting on the notion that being persons ourselves, we can more easily deal with personal forces because we have considerable experience and practice dealing with persons and also some degree of understanding of personal reresponses). That is, by personalizing nature, man can deal with it on a common plane. However, when the quality of holiness is added to the personal, it is no longer on a common plane with us. Perhaps it can be summarized this way: the unholy personal may *not threaten* or be *somewhat* threatening. The non-holy impersonal threatens *more*. The Holy personal threatens *most*. Stated another way, the unholy personal is most desirable, the non-holy, impersonal is less desirable; and the Holy personal is least desirable. We may understand and be able to cope with the unholy personal (men); but the Holy personal is more foreign and alien to us than the nonholy impersonal. We are, in effect, alienated by the alien. We have non or un-holiness in common with nature and differ at the point of personality. We have an analogous commonality with God at the point of personality but not at the point of holiness.

Thus the moral qualitative difference or strangeness that exists between man and God is greater than the ontological difference or strangeness that exists between man and nature. Simply stated man has more in common with nature than he does with God. His alienation toward God is greater than his alienation toward nature simply because there is a greater degree of "alienness" in God than there is in nature. We share creaturehood with nature but not with God. The qualitative difference between Creator and creature; God and man; the Unconditioned and the conditioned; the Holy and the unholy is an unbridgable chasm. The essential foreign element in God, the locus of His alien character, is to be found in His holiness.

## Human Reaction to the Holiness of Christ

The response of the disciples to Jesus in the episode of the calming of the sea is not atypical. A further illustration of the threatening character of Jesus may be seen in an incident involving Peter.

> And He saw two boats lying at the edge of the lake; but the fishermen had gotten out of them, and were washing their nets. And He got into one of the boats, which was Simon's, and asked him to put out a little way from the land. And He sat down and began teaching the multitudes from the boat. And when He had finished speaking, He said to Simon, "Put out into the deep water and let down your nets for a catch." And Simon answered and said, "Master, we worked hard all night and caught nothing, but at Your bidding I will let down the nets." And when they had done this, they enclosed a great quantity of fish; and their nets began to break; and they signaled to their partners in the other boat for them to come and help them. And they came, and filled both of the boats, so that they began to sink. But when Simon Peter saw that, he fell down at Jesus' feet, saying, "Depart from me, for I am a sinful man, O Lord!" For amazement had seized him and all his companions because of the catch of fish which they had taken. (Luke 5:3-9)

Here Peter's reaction to the power of Jesus over nature is somewhat startling. We can readily understand his astonishment at the work Jesus performed, but what was it that made him ask Jesus to leave?

Suddenly Jesus was unwelcome in the presence of Peter. Why? One would think that Peter's reaction would be to implore Jesus to sign on as a member of the crew. Any normal fisherman would be willing to make a man that can calm the sea and fill the nets on command, a full partner in his fishing enterprise. But Peter asked Him to leave. The reason he gives is not because Jesus messed his boat or tore his nets with all of the fish. He said, "Depart from me, for I am a sinful man!" Peter glimpsed more than naked power in His mighty act. Peter recognized the holiness present in Christ and the intrusion of the "Otherness" of the Holy made Peter uncommonly uncomfortable. Like Isaiah before him, Peter saw himself in contrast to Jesus, and he didn't like what he saw.

Perhaps no human being in the history of the world has received more praise and respect from men than Jesus of Nazareth. Even many who deny His claims to deity, etc., speak well of Him. John Gerstner has pointed out:

> The virgin reaction and all the subsequent reactions of the world to Jesus Christ is, then, that He is the ideal, the perfect man, the moral paragon of the race. I do not wish to gloss over the fact that not absolutely everyone has agreed with this verdict. I know that George Bernard Shaw spoke of a time in Christ's life when, as he said, Christ was not a Christian. I know that some have thought that Socrates died more nobly than Jesus: that others believe Him to have been morally surpassed. But the overwhelming testimony of the world is to the perfection, the incomparable perfection, of Jesus of Nazareth. The few exceptions could easily be shown to rest on fundamental misconceptions of certain things which Jesus said or did; and furthermore, the vast majority of those who do take exception usually think that some imagined fault is a failure

of Christ to be, as George Bernard Shaw said, a Christian! They seem to know of no higher standard by which to test Christ than the standard of Christ Himself.[13]

Other world religions have frequently spoken in glowing terms of Christ's moral excellence, and some have even sought to incorporate Him somehow into their own religious systems. Yet with all of these plaudits of the ages, the fact remains that Jesus was killed by His contemporaries. He is praised in the distance of time, but was intolerable to His contemporaries.

### The Threat of Moral Excellence

It is a common occurrence among social human beings that a person who manifests a superior excellence is resented by his contemporaries. The student who consistently breaks the curve of the academic grading system is frequently treated with quiet hostility by his classmates. Part of the now famous "Peter Principle" is that it is not only the super-incompetent person who is doomed to failure within the hierarchical structure of large corporations. The super-competent individual also faces the grim prospect of limited success by virtue of his very level of competence. The unusually competent person represents a threat not only to his peers but to his superiors as well and is frequently treated as *persona non grata.*

> These cases illustrate the fact that, in most hierarchies, *super-competence is more objectionable than incompetence.*
>
> Ordinary incompetence, as we have seen, is no cause for dismissal: it is simply a bar to promotion. Super-competence often leads to dismissal, *because it disrupts the hierarchy,* and thereby vi-

olates *the first commandment* of hierarchal life: the hierarchy must be preserved.[14]

Competency at a moral level is perhaps the most unwelcome kind of competency. The clergyman frequently functions as a symbol of moral competency. In the minds of many people the clergyman is a symbol of the sanctity of the church and is viewed with a kind of "innocence by association." The Dutch have a strange idiom to express this. When a group of people are engaged in vigorous and animated conversation which suddenly and abruptly halts momentarily, and an awkward silence prevails, someone will break the silence by uttering "*Loopt een dominee bij.*" (A minister walked by.) That is to say, because the appearance of a minister in real situations can inhibit free, spontaneous discourse and thus produce an awkward silence, any time an awkward silence occurs (even when no minister is near) the Dutchman says, "A minister walked by." That the presence of a clergyman can evoke a sense of inhibition and discomfort (no matter what he says or does) is common knowledge to any clergyman. I experience this phenomenon with regularity on the golf course. Invariably when another player fails to execute a good shot and in his frustration breaks forth with pointed expletives, he will turn to me and apologize for his momentary lapse into such cursing. The apologies come to me as if other men thought they were responsible to me for their cursing.

If clergymen or other people are imagined to be in a special class of moral excellence and are thus especially inhibiting and intimidating to their fellowmen, how much more inhibiting and intimidating was Christ? At the calming of the sea the final query of the disciples was, "What manner of man is this, that even the winds and the sea obey him?" What *kind* of man was Jesus? His contemporaries could not find an adequate class or category in which to pigeonhole Him. He manifested himself as the supreme *sui generis*. He was not only different; He was *unique*.

The unique moral excellence of Jesus was a massive threat to His contemporaries, particularly to those who were considered to be the moral elite of His day. It was the Pharisees (those "set apart" to righteousness) who were most hostile to Jesus. Though the popular masses hailed the Pharisees for their moral excellence, Jesus exposed them as hypocrites. He broke their curve, providing a new standard under which the old standard of morality dissolved. Jesus disintegrated the firm security of His contemporaries. When the Holy appeared, the pseudo-holy were exposed as being on the side of the unholy.

The holy and the pure are indirectly destructive forces, forces of disintegration. Absolute holiness, purity, and innocence cannot be tolerated because they are dangerous and destructive. Perhaps one of the most poignant paradigms of this phenomenon may be seen in the character of Lennie in Steinbeck's *Of Mice and Men*.

Lennie is portrayed as a man of enormous physical size with the mind and emotions of a child. His brute strength is exceeded in degree only by his simplistic innocence. Eking out an existence as a migrant worker, Lennie manifests a peculiar tender affection for little furry animals such as rabbits and mice. His concern for the well-being of these creatures is abnormal. He has an uncontrollable love for them that is expressed by holding them in his gargantuan hands and fondling and stroking them at length. However, Lennie's abnormal behavior frightens the animals, and in their panic they seek to squirm out of his grasp. In his innocence, Lennie grasps the creatures more tightly in an effort to show his love more deeply. However, Lennie is oblivious to his own strength; and in his effort to demonstrate his affection, he crushes the animals to death.

This peculiar quirk of Lennie's personality provides nothing more than a tolerable annoyance to Lennie's companion and guardian, George. No great harm is done until Lennie falls in love, not with another rabbit or mouse, but with a woman. One of the worker's wives tries to seduce Lennie, luring him on with soft hair which was made up in sausage curls. She invites Lennie to stroke her hair but panics when Lennie's stroke becomes too hard. Suddenly she seeks to leave him, turning on him with cruel insults. Bewildered, Lennie tries to hold her to show his deep love for her. Steinbeck writes:

> She struggled violently under his hands. Her feet battered on the hay and she writhed to be free; and from under Lennie's hand came a muffled screaming. Lennie began to cry with fright. "Oh! Please don't do none of that," he begged. "George gonna say I done a bad thing. He ain't gonna let me tend no rabbits." He moved his hand a little and her hoarse cry came out. Then Lennie grew angry. "Now don't," he said. "I don't want you to yell. You gonna get me in trouble jus' like George says you will. Now don't you do that." And she continued to struggle, and her eyes were wild with terror. He shook her then, and he was angry with her. "Don't you go yellin," he said, and he shook her; and her body flopped like a fish. And then she was still, for Lennie had broken her neck.[15]

With this incident Lennie's idiosyncracies were no longer tolerable. George whisked Lennie away with a posse in swift pursuit. Lennie had no real understanding of the enormity of his crime. He babbled repeatedly like a child, "I done a bad thing...." Finally with the posse at their heels, George pointed beyond the river to an imaginary farm where there awaited for Lennie a multitude of rabbits, mice, puppies and other furry creatures. As Lennie stood transfixed by the conjured vision, contemplating endless hours of showing his unreserved affection, George calmly and deliberately blew his brains out with a revolver. When the posse arrived one of the men reflected to George, "Never you mind.... A guy got to sometimes."

Lennie was a freak. His abnormal affection made him intolerable to society. His love was the kind that was both tender and brutal. He destroyed the objects of his affection because he loved them more than they wanted to be loved. The power of his love evoked fear in them and consequently they sought with all of their might to flee from them. Many have seen in Steinbeck's "Lennie" a dramatic Christ-like figure. The parallels are obvious. Abnormal love cannot be tolerated as it leaves man and beast in a state of traumatic discomfort.

## Cosmic Claustrophobia

Another dimension of the holiness of God which provokes a negative human response is the dimension of God's glory. The concept of God's glory is inseparably related to holiness. In Biblical categories, the glory of God is expressed in Old Testament terms of *kabod* and New Testament terms of *doxa*. The corresponding Latin term for this concept is the word *dignitas* from which our English word "dignity" derives.

*The Kabod of God.* In the Old Testament the term

*Kabod* is used in close connection with the word *qodesh* (holy). Though the two are closely related, they can be distinguished. Jacob says of God's *Kabod*:

> This glory is what God possesses in his own right, it is a kind of totality of qualities which make up his divine power; it has a close affinity with the holiness which is of the nature of deity and it is a visible extension for the purpose of manifesting holiness to men. Whether it be manifest in the sphere of creation, history or the cultus, it is always, to use Bengel's particularly happy expression, uncovered holiness (*die aufgedeckte Heiligkeit*) or, to express it in more picturesque language which takes account of the concrete aspect of *Kabod*, "the incandescent ectoplasm of his invisible spirit." [16]

The root meaning of *Kabod* is "weighty," "heavy," or "important." Kittel says Kabod is "something weighty or impressive, a *gravitas* which constitutes man's place in society, and therefore an anthropological term." [17] Thus there is a sense in which the word glory is used to describe man as well as God. Just as we speak frequently of the "dignity" of man, so the Bible speaks of man's glory. The glory of man is located in his importance and prestige in the cosmos.

When the glory of man is related to the glory of God, there is a marked contrast. In the context of the glory of God, human glory is dwarfed by comparison. The weightiness of divine glory presses in upon man, threatening to crowd him out. Kittel maintains:

> If in relation to man *kabod* denotes that which makes him impressive and demands recognition, whether in terms of material possessions or striking *gravitas*,

in relation to God it implies that which makes God impressive to man, the force of His self-manifestation.[18]

Throughout the Old Testament the glory of God represents an awesome manifestation of God's being. The image of the thunderstorm is frequently used to point to God's glory. Glory is always somewhat veiled by theophany. Direct access to glory is denied. God's glory is glimpsed here in the pillar of cloud and there in the flaming sword; but an unveiled, unobscured vision cannot be endured by human eyes.

Even Moses, in his privileged position of being the mediator of the Old Covenant, is not permitted to gaze directly at the glory of God. We read in the narrative of Exodus:

> Then Moses said, "I pray Thee, show me Thy glory!" And He said, "I Myself will make all My goodness pass before you, and will proclaim the name of the Lord before you; and I will be gracious to whom I will be gracious, and will show compassion on whom I will show compassion." But He said, "You cannot see My face, for no man can see me and live!" Then the Lord said, "Behold, there is a place by Me, and you shall stand there on the rock; and it will come about, while My glory is passing by, that I will put you in the cleft of the rock and cover you with My hand until I have passed by. Then I will take My hand away and you shall see My back, but my face shall not be seen." (Ex. 33:18-23)

Here Moses is allowed to see the back of God, but a direct frontal view of His glory is prohibited.

Even this direct viewing of God's glory presents problems for Moses as he returns to speak with the people of Israel. When Moses descended from his encounter with God on Mt. Sinai, his face shone in a way that reflected the glory of God. The sight of Moses terrified the people:

> So when Aaron and all the sons of Israel saw Moses, behold, the skin of his face shone, and they were afraid to come near him. . . . When Moses had finished speaking with them, he put a veil over his face. But whenever Moses went in before the Lord to speak with Him, he would take off the veil until he came out; and whenever he came out and spoke to the sons of Israel what he had been commanded, the sons of Israel would see the face of Moses, that the skin of Moses' face shone. So Moses would replace the veil over his face until he went in to speak with Him. (Ex. 34:30-35)

In the New Testament the concept of the glory of God is rendered by the Greek δόξα from which the English term "doxology" derives. One of the astonishing factors in the New Testament is the way in which the term is used in connection with Jesus. Kittel says of this, "The New Testament usage itself takes a decisive step by using in relation to Christ a word which was used in relation to God." [19] John says concerning Jesus:

> And the Word became flesh, and dwelt among us, and we beheld His glory, glory as of the only begotten from the Father, full of grace and truth. (John 1:14)

Perhaps what John refers to in his prologue in terms of beholding the glory of Christ is the Transfiguration. The account of this episode in the life of Jesus is a very puzzling one. What is clearly implied by the text, however, is that the disciples were afforded an unparalleled glimpse of the glory of Christ. Luke says:

> And some eight days after these sayings, it came about that He took along Peter and John and James, and went up to the mountain to pray. And while He was praying, the appearance of His face became different, and His clothing became white and

gleaming. And behold, two men were talking with Him; and they were Moses and Elijah, who, appearing in glory, were speaking of His departure which He was about to accomplish at Jerusalem.... And while He was saying this, a cloud formed and began to overshadow them; and they were afraid as they entered the cloud. (Luke 9:28-34)

The appearance of Christ in glory is an awesome thing. The Biblical writers speak of the "weight of His glory." This weightiness is the subject of the churches' doxology and of the pagans' hostility. In the great Christological controversies of the fourth century, the church saw an inseparable relationship between doxology and the confession of the deity of Christ. Out of the struggle with Arianism the *gloria patra* emerged as a "fight-song" for the trinitarians. The song contained the words:

Glory be to the Father,
And to the Son, And to
The Holy Ghost . . .

The threefold ascription of glory was a confessional formula for the Trinity.

Throughout the history of the church the glory of God has remained as a focal point of praise and adoration. To the non-Christian, however, it has been the focus of cosmic claustrophobia. That is the weightiness and heaviness of God have been felt as a crushing power which men would prefer to "make light of." The mocking of God is seen Biblically as a failure to take seriously His dignity—His *Kabod*—His glory. Thus the weightiness of God's glory is an integral part of the trauma of holiness.

CHAPTER 6

## God and Nakedness

One of the most fascinating arguments against the existence of God ever developed has come from the pen of Jean Paul Sartre. Sartre has manifested an uncanny ability to penetrate the interior dimension of human feeling and reaction to life situations that touch on human personality. Developing a phenomenological view of man and the world, Sartre reverses the order of classical idealism, rationalism and essentialism with his famous slogan, *"existence précède l'essence."*

With the notion of the priority of existence over essence, Sartre takes issue with all who seek an understanding of men by understanding the particular in light of the universal; the individual in light of the group; or the species in light of the genus. He begins his critique of theism at the point of the Christian notion of creation of man by divine providence. If God produces men in a similar fashion to the method employed by a human artisan, then He proceeds to create "man" according to some preconceived plan or idea of "humanness" to which the created reality must correspond or conform. Hence in creation man's "existence" would be threatened by the priority of "essence" as it flows from the consciousness of God.[1]

In analyzing human existence, Sartre roots the uniqueness of man in his being a subject rather than an object. Man's existence-in-consciousness (*le pour-soi*) cannot be reduced to a thing (*l'en-soi*). It is precisely at the point of man's subjectivity that Sartre offers a rather unique critique of the existence of God. Beyond the ontological objections Sartre raises, he introduces the notion of the "look" or the "gaze" that threatens the existence of men by seeking to reduce them to the level of objects.

Perhaps no philosopher has provided a more cogent analysis of the existential dynamics of the experience of being "looked at" than Sartre. In *Being and Nothingness* Sartre devotes an entire section to the experience of "The Look." In this section he displays a genius level of introspection, using as his basic paradigm the scenario of a man who looks through a key-hole at someone, and is caught in his act of voyeurism by another. He narrates the situation by saying:

> But all of a sudden I hear footsteps in the hall. Someone is looking at me! What does this mean? It means that I am suddenly affected in my being and that essential modifications appear in my structure-modifications which I can apprehend and fix conceptually by means of the reflective *cogito*.[2]

The experience of being beneath the gaze or the look of the Other includes possible elements of shame, fear and/or pride. Sartre devotes most of his attention to the experience which he calls "shame—consciousness." This shame does not take place in a vacuum. Rather shame is experienced in the presence of the Other. In this experience my subjectivity is reduced to objectivity as I become the object of the gaze or scrutiny of the Other. I lose mastery of the situation and experience shame. Sartre says:

> Similarly shame is only the original feeling of having my being *outside*, engaged in another being and as such without any defense, illuminated by the absolute light which emanates from a pure subject. Shame is the consciousness of being irremediably what I always was: "in suspense"—that is, in the mode of the "not yet" or of the "already-no-longer." Pure shame is not a feeling of being this or that guilty object but in general of being *an* object; that is, of *recognizing myself* in this degraded, fixed, and dependent being which I am for the Other. Shame is the feeling of an *original fall*, not because of the fact that I may have committed this or that particular fault but simply that I have "fallen" into the world in the midst of things and that I need the mediation of the Other in order to be what I am.[3]

Thus, for Sartre, "shame-consciousness" is bound up with being in the presence of the Other. "Shame is a unitary apprehension with three dimensions: *I* am ashamed of *myself* before the *Other*."[4] Coming under the gaze of another is dangerous business as my subjectivity is at stake, and my freedom from shame is threatened.

Sartre dramatizes the threatening character of coming under the gaze of the Other in his play *No Exit*. The play involved four characters confined to a room in which no mirrors are available, and the people are left to the experience of communicating with each other. The setting of the drawing room without articles of torture or punishment depicts Sartre's portrait of hell. What appears as a pleasant setting for social intercourse finally manifests an environment of mutual destruction. The oft-quoted punch-line of the play is uttered by Garcin:

> This bronze. (Strokes it thoughtfully.) Yes, now's the moment: I'm looking at this thing on the mantel-

piece, and I understand that I'm in hell. I tell you, everything's been thought out beforehand. They knew I'd stand at the fireplace stroking this thing of bronze, with all those eyes intent on me. Devouring me. (*He swings round abruptly.*) What? Only two of you? I thought there were more; many more. (*Laughs.*) So this is hell. I'd never have believed it. You remember all we were told about the torture-chambers, the fire and brimstone, the "burning marl." Old wives' tales! There's no need for red-hot pokers. Hell is—other people! [5]

"Hell is other people!"—this line is seen as the climactic moment of the play. Yet frequently a more subtle point of the drama is lost by the revelation of Garcin. It is found in the final stage directive of the text:

*(They slump onto their respective sofas. A long silence. Their laughter dies away and they gaze at each other.)* [6]

If Sartre finds the experience of being subjected to the gaze of other people repugnant, how much more hellish does he regard the gaze of God? For Sartre, God implies not so much an "Unmoved Mover" as an "Unviewed Viewer." That is, God is the ultimate Other who has the capacity of omniscience, whereby He keeps everyone beneath His gaze, while at the same time no one may gaze at Him. God plays the game of the cosmic voyeur who has no fear of being discovered at His celestial key-hole by another. Beneath God's gaze we are all reduced to absolute objects and have our humanity destroyed. Thus, for Sartre, if man exists as a subject, God cannot exist.

### Existential Self-Awareness

Analysis of the phenomenon of self-awareness is not unique with Sartre. It has been the subject of considerable interest in modern culture as indicated by the popular receptivity of Julius Fast's book, *Body Language*. In this volume the author provides an analysis of ways in which human beings indulge in nonverbal communication. Numerous variations of the position of the eyelid and eyebrow, the posture of standing at ease, and the dynamics of other bodily gestures are all noted as part of man's tools of communication. Of special interest, however, is the nature and the function of the human stare.

Fast points out the difference between the "acceptable" and the "unacceptable" stare. One can stare for long periods at monkeys in the zoo, or at paintings in a museum, with impunity. But to stare at a man in public with the same intensity or duration that is acceptable in the case of monkeys is to risk a bloody nose. Our cultural mores consider prolonged staring at human beings as involving an exercise in discourtesy. Though "eye-contact" is a necessary component of social conversation, there remains a thin line between the friendly duration and intensity of such eye-contact and the threatening "stare." If a glance is held too long it can provoke embarrassment or even hostility.

Stated simply, the stare is appropriate for objects, but not for personal subjects. To be the victim of a stare is to be threatened by de-personalization. To become an object under the gaze of another provokes discomfort. We speak of "feeling" someone's eyes upon us, of people "looking through us." Women complain of the male stare as making them feel as though they are being undressed, etc. In acknowledging strangers, we must avoid staring at them, and yet we must also avoid ignoring them. To treat them as people rather than objects, we use a deliberate and polite inattention. We look at them long enough to make it quite clear that we see them, and then we immediately look away. We are saying in body language, "I know you are there," and a moment later we add, "but I would not dream of intruding on your privacy." [7]

As one frequently involved in public speaking, I am aware of the threatening character of the stare. In a public speaking situation it is important for the speaker to maintain eye-contact with his audience. Yet in that eye-contact he must avoid staring at a single person. If the Sunday morning preacher delivered his sermon by staring at a single member of the congregation throughout the duration of his sermon, he would be apt to lose a parishioner. On the other hand, it is permissible for the members of the audience to keep their eyes fixed upon the speaker. This state of affairs can easily provoke existential self-awareness, especially if the speaker is given to the extemporaneous form of address. In my own experience I discover that as I am speaking, my mind is concentrating on what I am about to say next. However, if in the course of the address I notice someone in the audience peering at me intently, I can easily lose my train of thought via self-awareness. If I stop to consider that the people are analyzing not only my message but me, paying attention not only to my words but also to my mannerisms, clothing, hair-style, etc., I could not only lose my train of thought but inevitably go stark, raving mad. Every speaker must struggle, either consciously or unconsciously, to block from his mind the threatening character of being subjected to the scrutiny of the collective gaze of his audience.

The above illustrations suffice to indicate the complex dimensions of the phenomenon of the stare. The stare can make us uncomfortable. We can sense via the stare a reification of our personalities, a loss of humanness. We can "feel" or experience a sense of invasion of our privacy. In a word we can feel *exposed* or reduced to nakedness. Clothes, shower-curtains, door, and window-shades are only a few modern conveniences that testify to some level of human need to protect one's nakedness from the gaze of another person.

## The Nakedness Motif of Western Culture

Nudity and semi-nudity are concerns of some fascination in the Western world. The rise in popularity of X-rated films, topless waitresses, go-go dancers, the bikini, male and female nude center-folds, Woodstock-type festivals, etc., herald an almost adolescent preoccupation with nakedness. Yet shower-curtains and window shades remain household staples. On the one hand we see a desire to view nudity or be naked, and on the other a desire to remain covered. Why the mystique over nudity?

Desmond Morris begins his best-selling work, *The Naked Ape*, by saying:

> There are one hundred and ninety-three living species of monkeys and apes. One hundred and ninety-two of them are covered with hair. The exception is a naked-ape self-named *Homo sapiens*.[8]

Thus from a zoological perspective, considering man as a primate, Morris pinpoints the uniqueness of man in his nakedness.

In less dramatic fashion, the aspect of nakedness has figured widely in modern man's attempt at self-understanding. In psychological environs, the nude-therapy session has emerged as a frequent motif of sensitivity-training techniques. People are encouraged to experience a high level of "vulnerability" by exposing themselves physically to others in the group of a context of trust. "Being open" and "sharing" or "revealing" one's innermost feelings has been connected with nudity. To shed clothes (the physical covering) is to expose not only the body, but to remove the defenses or the "covering" of the human psyche. The small-group movement in popular religious circles has also stressed such "vulnerability" or "openness" as being of therapeutic value to the soul. The hope of an experience of forgiveness or acceptance followed by small-group confession has been widespread.

Some people who have experienced such vulnerability sessions either in a secular or church situation have testified enthusiastically to feelings of liberation—of being released from the curse of living in a state of concealment. Others have testified to experiencing great trauma from such self-exposure.

There remains a kind of paradoxical attitude among many people to the matter of nakedness. A kind of collective ambivalence seems to be manifest in our culture about nudity. On the one hand, there is an enormous desire to view the naked body and at the same time to conceal it. There is the exhilarating feeling of liberation that often accompanies the act of undressing, yet at the same time a sense of shame or embarrassment if caught unexpectedly in a nude state.

This paradoxical character of nakedness is reflected in Kierkegaard's notion of man as the *Homo Absconditus*. For centuries theologians have operated with the concept of the *Deus Absconditus*, i.e., that aspect of God which remains hidden and obscured from human knowledge, that aspect of God which remains "unrevealed." But Kierkegaard calls attention to the need of an *Absconditus* dimension of man. On the one hand, Kierkegaard is sharply critical of the person who lives merely on the "aesthetic" or "spectator" plane of life, operating within the context of the concealment of a masquerade. For that person Kierkegaard demands a radical "unmasking" to expose the chimera. He says in *Either/or:*

> Life is a masquerade, you explain, and for you this is inexhaustible material for amusement; and so far, no one has succeeded in knowing you; for every revelation you make is always an illusion, it is only in this way you are able to breathe and prevent people from pressing importunately upon you and obstructing your respiration. Your occupation consists in preserving your hiding-place, and that you succeed in doing, for your mask is the most enigmatical of all. In fact you are nothing; you are merely a relation to others, and what you are you are by virtue of this relation. To a fond shepherdess you hold out a lanquishing hand, and instantly you are masked in all possible bucolic sentimentality. A reverend spiritual father you deceive with a brotherly kiss, etc. You yourself are nothing, an enigmatic figure on whose brow is inscribed Either/or—"For this," you say, "is my motto, and these words are not, as the grammarians believe, disjunctive conjunctions; no, they belong inseparately together and therefore ought to be written as one word, inasmuch as in their union they constitute an interjection which I shout at mankind, just as boys shout 'Hep' after a Jew." [9]

In this scathing critique of the dishonest spectator, Kierkegaard hurls a challenge:

> Do you not know that there comes a midnight hour when everyone has to throw off his mask? Do you believe that life will always let itself be mocked? Do you think you can slip away a little before midnight in order to avoid this? Or are you not terrified by it? I have seen men in real life who so long deceived others that at last their true nature could not reveal itself: I have seen men who played hide and seek so long that at last madness through

them obtruded disgustingly upon others their secret thoughts which hitherto they had proudly concealed .... In every man there is something which to a certain degree prevents him from becoming perfectly transparent to himself; and this may be the case in so high a degree, he may be so inexplicably woven into relationships of life which extend far beyond himself that he almost cannot reveal himself. But he who cannot reveal himself cannot love, and he who cannot love is the most unhappy man of all.[10]

Thus Kierkegaard sees self-concealment as being inevitably self-destructive. The ability to expose or reveal oneself is the *sine qua non* of the ability to love.

With such a strong indictment of self-concealment and the passionate plea to move beyond the stadium of the aesthetic, we might jump to the conclusion that Kierkegaard is writing a brief for total self-exposure. It sometimes sounds as if he is asking us to "let it all hang out," to jump into a state of absolute vulnerability in a spirit of reckless abandon. But such is not the case. Kierkegaard, the "Gadfly," did not go about Denmark naked. Though he called for living in a passionate state of high-level risk, he preserved an island of hiddenness for himself and for all men. Man can never escape a certain measure of "existential solitude," nor should he. Solitude affords a place of hiddenness that is necessary for the human subject. Kierkegaard writes:

> On the other hand, he often feels a need of solitude, which for him is a vital necessity—sometimes like breathing, at other times like sleeping. The fact that he feels this vital necessity more than other men is also a sign that he has a deeper nature. Generally the need of solitude is a sign that there is spirit in a man after all, and it is a measure

for what spirit there is. The purely twaddling inhuman and too-human men are to such a degree without feeling for the need of solitude that, like a certain species of social birds, (the so-called love birds), they promptly die if for an instant they have to be alone. As this little child must be put to sleep by a lullaby, so these men need the tranquilizing hum of society before they are able to eat, drink, sleep, pray, fall in love, etc. But in ancient times as well as in the Middle Ages people were aware of the need of solitude and had respect for what it signifies. In the constant sociability of our age people shudder at solitude to such a degree that they know no other use to put it to but (oh, admirable epigram!) as a punishment for criminals. But after all it is a fact that in our age it is a crime to have spirit, so it is natural that such people, the lovers of solitude, are included in the same class with criminals.[11]

Kierkegaard sees a paradoxical dimension to human self-revelation. Analogous to the relationship in God between the notion of the *Deus Revelatus* and the *Deus Absconditus* in the act of human revelation that comes by indirect communication. Zuidema summarizes Kierkegaard by saying:

No single mode of expression is able to reveal or disclose the inner and individual character of the existence or being of the human self. All expression, all communication is in its very nature a withdrawal, a mystery, a hiddenness. Expression and communication distort that which one would express. This cannot be otherwise. For communication, even verbal communication, is an externalization, an objectivization and generalization. The individual becoming of internal and free existence does not disclose itself to objective discursive thought. Nor does it reveal or disclose its own intimacy through the self-revelation of the spoken word. It does not permit its self-disclosure through this spoken word. Revelation is concealment. The individual is inexpressible and imperceptible. Man lives incognito throughout his life.[12]

Thus we find irony, paradox and ambivalence in Western man's idea of nakedness/clothedness and concealment/openness. To "reveal" is closely linked with the act of "unveiling" of either body or mind. This ambivalence is attested by a multitude of sources ranging from the attitudes displayed from the class B-movie and the tabloid, to the sophisticated treatment by the genius of a Kierkegaard or a Sartre.

### The Biblical Motif of Nakedness

The theme of nakedness plays a remarkable role in Biblical literature. The importance of the nakedness motif is often overlooked and consequently suffers from woeful neglect. The state of nakedness is closely linked with the Hebraic concept of "knowing" in a complex variety of ways. We will explore by way of Biblical reconnaissance, the motif of nakedness in an attempt to relate its significance to Sartre's notion of the "glance" and Kierkegaard's notion of *homo absconditus*.

The word γυμνός (gumnos) is used Biblically in both a literal and figurative sense. In its literal sense it is capable of being translated as "naked," "unclothed," "badly clothed" or "stripped by force." In its figurative usage the term γυμνός is capable of a wider variety of nuances. Such ideas as "unconcealed," "disclosed," or "manifest" are conveyed by the figurative sense of nakedness. The state of the soul apart from the body is described by the Greeks as a "naked state." Hadrian at his death addressed his *animula nudula*.) Nakedness is mentioned in antiquity as part of the torment of the damned. In the Samaritan liturgy for the eve of the Day of Atonement the *goyim* will be raised naked, whereas the righteous will rise again with clothes. Finally, there is the sense in which nakedness describes the state of the soul or inner man that is without preparation for the day of judgment.[13]

### Noah's Nakedness

One of the most fascinating and puzzling narratives of the Pentateuch is the account of the episode of Ham's violation of his father, Noah, by means of looking at his nakedness. The account reads:

> Then Noah began farming and planted a vineyard. And he drank of the wine and became drunk, and uncovered himself inside his tent. And Ham, the father of Canaan, saw the nakedness of his father, and told his two brothers outside. But Shem and Japheth took a garment and laid it upon both their shoulders and walked backward and covered the nakedness of their father; and their faces were turned away, so that they did not see their father's nakedness. When Noah awoke from his wine, he knew what his youngest son had done to him. So he said, "Cursed be Canaan; a servant of servants he shall be to his brothers." He also said, "Blessed be the Lord, the God of Shem; and let Canaan be his servant. May God enlarge Japheth, and let him dwell in the tents of Shem; and let Canaan be his servant." (Gen. 9:20-27)

In this strange account the descendants of Ham receive the curse of their patriarchal ancestor Noah because Ham looked on his father's nakedness. Conversely, Shem and Japheth receive the patriarchal blessings because they refused to gaze upon their nude father and because they provided a covering for him. Notice in the passage that the "sin" of Ham is not that he looked upon his father's drunkenness, nor that he made sport or ridicule of his father's condition. The sin is in the *looking* at the nakedness of his father.

To receive the patriarchal curse is indeed a serious matter for the Jew of antiquity. By contemporary standards, Noah's judgment seems outrageous. To curse your son because he looks at your naked body seems like a measure of cruel and unjust punishment. Justice appears mutilated by a punishment that is more severe than the crime. How can we make sense out of this enigmatic narrative that violates our modern sense of crime and punishment? Perhaps some insight can be gained by a broader view of Biblical attitudes toward *nakedness*.

### The Old Testament Law

The Levitical Law gives detailed prohibitions and prescriptions for punishment concerning nakedness. A sampling of the law provides the following casuistic applications of the general prohibition of adultery:

> If there is a man who lies with his father's wife, he has uncovered his father's nakedness; both of them shall surely be put to death, their bloodguiltiness is upon them. (Lev. 20:11)

In this passage incest involves an uncovering of the father's nakedness. That is, the nakedness of the husband is identified by law as being equated with the nakedness of the wife. To uncover a man's wife is seen as a stripping of the man himself. The same attitude of uncovering is indicated with respect to uncle, brother, and other blood relatives (Lev. 20:20-21). Again we read:

> If there is a man who takes his sister, his father's daughter of his mother's daughter, so that he sees her nakedness and she sees his nakedness, it is a disgrace; and they shall be cut off in the sight

of the sons of the people. He has uncovered his sister's nakedness; he bears his guilt. (Lev. 20:17)

You shall also not uncover the nakedness of your mother's sister or of your father's sister, for such a one has made naked his blood relative; they shall bear their guilt. (Lev. 20:19)

From these samplings from the Old Testament Law it is obvious that the Jew of antiquity took the matter of nakedness very seriously.

Beyond the Levitical Law concern is often expressed for the threatening and dreadful character of nakedness. In the midst of unspeakable misery Job rents his garments and shaves his head crying: "Naked I came from my mother's womb, and naked I shall return there" (Job 1:21). Amos pronounces God's judgment on Israel by saying:

"Flight will perish from the swift, and the stalwart will not strengthen his power, nor the mighty man save his life. He who grasps the bow will not stand his ground; the swift of foot will not escape, nor will he who rides the horse save his life. Even the bravest among the warriors will flee naked in that day," declares the Lord. (Amos 2:14-16)

Again nakedness is seen as a thing of doom, used by God as a means of punishment for the wicked. To be "sent naked away" is to be stripped to the point of humiliation and emptiness.

## Nakedness in the New Testament

The concern for the threatening character of nakedness is not limited to the Old Testament world. It appears frequently in the New Testament. Christ promises blessings to those who fed Him when He was hungry, provided drink and hospitality when He was thirsty and a stranger, visited Him in prison and clothed Him when He was *naked*. When queried about this by His disciples, Jesus declared, "Truly I say to you, to the extent that you did it to one of these brothers of mine, even the least of them, you did it to me" (Matt. 25:40). Jesus makes the clothing of the naked a priority in the establishing of the Kingdom of God.

The question of Jesus' clothing at the time of His crucifixion is unclear. His garments were divided among His executioners but the temporal sequence is obscure. The implication is, however, that part of the ignominy of Christ's humiliation is that He was crucified naked, being made a public spectacle. The parallel with the lament of the Psalmist is obvious:

> For dogs have surrounded me;
> A band of evildoers had encompassed me;
> They pierced my hands and my feet.
> I can count all my bones.
> They *look*, they *stare* at me;
> They divide my garments among them,
> And for my clothing they cast lots. (Ps. 22:16-18)

The writer of the Apocalypse records the warning of Christ to the Church of Laodicea:

> Because you say, "I am rich, and have become wealthy, and have need of nothing," and you do not know that you are wretched and miserable and poor and blind and naked, I advise you to buy from me gold refined by fire, that you may become rich, and white garments, that you may clothe yourself, and that the shame of your nakedness may not be revealed, and eyesalve to anoint your eyes, that you may see. (Rev. 3:17-18)

Again in chapter 16 Christ says, "Blessed is the one who stays awake and keeps his garments, lest he walk about naked and men see his shame" (Rev. 16:15).

The above-mentioned passages indicate clearly that nakedness is not a desirable state. Shame, humiliation, ignominy, and doom are associated with the naked state. But the question remains, why all the fuss about nakedness? Why is there such a correlation between nudity and humiliation? Why is it that to be unclothed is to be reduced to ignominy? The answer to these questions must be found in the context of the Biblical account of the Fall of man.

### Nakedness and The Fall

In the Genesis narrative of the creation of man and woman, we have a very succinct summation given; perhaps a bit too succinct, leaving the reader with a mild sense of the abrupt:

> And the Lord God fashioned into a woman the rib which He had taken from the man, and brought her to the man. And the man said, "This is now bone of my bones, and flesh of my flesh; she shall be called Woman, because she was taken out of Man." For this cause a man shall leave his father and his mother, and shall cleave to his wife, and they shall become one flesh. (Gen. 2:22-24)

At this point the creation narrative seems to reach a conclusion with the sanctification of the institution of marriage culminating in the union of man and woman. Yet the narrative does not cease at this expected point of climax but seems to tack on a kind of "concluding unscientific postscript" which sounds a bit foreign to the context of the narrative. Almost as an afterthought we read the statement, "And the man and his wife were both naked and were not ashamed" (Gen. 2:25).

"Naked and unashamed?" It sounds like an afterthought, but it is obviously more than that. This description of the primordial couple in the state of innocence is a crucial transition to the narrative that follows: the narrative of the Fall. The author of Genesis provides us with a gripping study in contrast which focuses on the words, "naked and unashamed."

The account of the Fall of man rehearses the episode of the temptation proffered by the serpent. When Adam and Eve succumb to the temptation and experience sin, their first reaction was a reaction to their own nakedness. The narrative reads:

> Then the eyes of both of them were opened, and they knew that they were naked; and they sewed fig leaves together and made themselves loin coverings. And they heard the sound of the Lord God walking in the garden in the cool of the day, and the man and his wife hid themselves from the presence of the Lord God among the trees of the garden. (Gen. 3:7-8)

Here the consciousness of Adam and Eve was not immediately directed towards thoughts of the serpent, or the tree, or even God. Their eyes were opened (as the serpent suggested they would be), but what they saw was their own nakedness. But they had not been previously blind. It wasn't that now they experienced the empirical power of visual perception for the first time. Adam could see the nakedness of Eve very plainly before the Fall. Nor was he blinded to the observation of his own body. The "opening of their eyes" is of course a figurative description of an awareness of shame. Perhaps, precisely what Sartre describes as "shame-consciousness." Where previously they delighted in the sound of God as He walked in the cool of the day, now they were terrified by that sound. Where they previously stood secure and totally unembarrassed beneath the gaze of God, now they desperately sought refuge from the sight. Man's nakedness being once a sign of the glory of innocence becomes his greatest disgrace. Luther remarks:

> Similarly, man does not realize that the glory of nakedness was lost through sin. The fact that Adam and Eve walked about naked was their greatest adornment before God and all the creatures. Now, after sin, we not only shun the glance of men when we are naked; but we are even bashful in our own presence....[14]

The relationship between physical nakedness and spiritual exposure is clear in this passage. In hiding their nakedness from the vision of God, Adam and Eve were hiding themselves.

The rest of the narrative tells of God searching for His creatures, calling out to Adam, "Where are you?" Adam responds, "I heard the sound of Thee in the garden, and I was afraid because I was naked; so I hid myself." Under the interrogation of his Maker, Adam uses a desperately contrived "cover-up" ploy. He claims that he is hiding because he is afraid and that the reason for his fear is his nakedness. A perfectly "natural" explanation for the original act of *Homo Absconditus*; an explanation that sufficed only until God raised the next question, "Who told you that you were naked?"

The ploy failed and Adam's sin was exposed to the gaze of God. For Adam and his progeny the trauma was unforgettable. Even Sartre remarks:

> Modesty and in particular the fear of being surprised in a state of nakedness are only a symbolic specification of original shame; the body symbolizes here our defenseless state as objects. To put on clothes is to hide one's object-state; it is to claim the right of seeing without being seen; that is, to be pure subject. This is why the Biblical symbol of the fall after the original sin is the fact that Adam

and Eve "know that they are naked." The reaction to shame will consist exactly in apprehending as an object the one who apprehended my own object-state.[15]

With the experience of sin comes the awareness of shame-in-nakedness. Throughout Biblical history the motif is carried on. Yet some startling things take place in the Paradise situation that are frequently overlooked. With the sin comes judgment, punishment, and expulsion from Eden. Man leaves the Garden under the curse of God. But he does not leave naked!

In light of the indictment of God for the act of transgression, we might expect that God would rudely drag Adam from his hiding place, tear away the fig-leaf in an act of divine fury, and condemn the man to a life of utter exposure and shame. We might justly expect God to reduce His creature to the unprotected state of pure objectivity, being constantly exposed to His wrathful gaze and the gaze of all creation. But He does not. The judgment is real; indeed, it is devastating—but it is not ultimate. We read in Genesis 3:21, "And the Lord God made garments of skin for Adam and his wife, and clothed them." In a word, God provided a "hiding-place" for His embarrassed creature. God beheld Adam's nakedness and like Shem and Japheth did for Noah, God covered that nakedness. Beneath the gaze of God Adam found redemption, not annihilation. Adam experienced not only the stare of judgment but the benevolent gaze of love.

## Being Known of God

The threat of exposure, of being caught naked, is inseparably related to the very real and ominous threat of being known as we are. Again ambivalence is characteristic of the human attitude toward being known. We go to extraordinary pains to hide those things about ourselves of which we are ashamed; yet at the same time we yearn for a place of refuge where we can be fully known without fear, where we can be naked and unashamed. The thought of being known is both terrifying and desirable. It is desirable to be at peace with our own self-understanding but fearful that the truth will bring only judgment and disapproval. The thought that "hell is other people" is not the isolated insight of a tormented playwright but the collective fear of Adam's seed.

The ambivalence of being known is aptly visible in the standard procedure of the courting process of American youth that progresses from the encounter of the first date to the moment of truth in the honeymoon suite. The first date is captured in the symbol of the "first impression." The magic of hair spray, mascara, deodorant, etc., is plied in a massive effort to conceal ugliness and portray beauty. The conversation is cautious, guarded from being too revealing. Making a good impression is the order of the day. But if the first date is successful and the relationship progresses to a more serious level, a crisis state is soon reached. The crisis comes when the person realizes that the other is responding warmly and the question begins to plague the mind, "Is she responding to me or to the image I've carefully projected?" What follows is the *trial*. Little bits of hidden areas are revealed and confessions of sins committed "long ago and far away" are made. (I am reminded of the preacher who after admonishing his parishioners for their current sins, was quick to show his humility and solidarity with human weakness by confessing that he wasn't perfect, noting from the pulpit that he had "stolen" his father's car, without permission, when he was fourteen years old! Hardly a painful confession.) If the trial of "remote confession" is successful, then the tyro-lover moves closer to the rim of authentic self-exposure. What is sought is the experience of loving and being loved in truth rather than concealment. Some, however, as Kierkegaard has observed, never pass the trial as their fear of exposure is so great that it outweighs their desire to be known and loved. Some even marry but only as a way of gaining a ticket to a perpetual game of hide and seek.

So it is with being known of God. Who isn't threatened, indeed intimidated, by the notion of an all-knowing deity who acts as a cosmic "Big Brother"? To consider the thought that my life knows no secrets from the penetrating eye of God may be most discouraging. Yet I want to be known; I need to be known: Ambivalence.

This ambivalence is clearly manifest in Biblical history. Let David be the paradigm. After his heinous crime against Bathsheba which included the indirect murder of her husband, David had so deceived himself about the extent of his guilt that he didn't even recognize himself in Nathan's parable until Nathan boldly declared, "Thou art the man!" David's deception had reached the level of self-deception. When the revelation came and David was exposed, it was painful for him. He cried out in contrition: "For I know my transgressions, and my sin is ever before me. Against Thee, and Thee only, I have sinned, and done what is evil in Thy sight" (Ps. 51). Here David acknowledges the reality of that guilt and notes two very important factors. First he notes that the sin is *ever* before him. It hounds him and pursues him. He sees it wherever he goes. He cannot rid himself of the memory. Like

Lady Macbeth, the spot is indelible. Second, he notes that he has done evil in the sight of God. Thus, David not only sees his sin but he realizes it hasn't escaped the notice of God. So painful is that realization that David engages in hyperbole by saying, "Against Thee, and Thee only, I have sinned." That may be true in an ultimate sense, but in the human context of David's guilt it is hyperbole. He sinned against Bathsheba, Uriah, his generals, his wives, and against the whole nation of Israel by using the power of the crown for his own gain in adultery. David violated a lot of people. His shame before the nation was great but not worthy of comparison with his shame before God.

David knows that God sees his sin and this is unbearable. He cries: "Let the bones which Thou has broken rejoice. Hide Thy face from my sins, and blot out all my iniquities." So threatening is the gaze of God that David begs God to cover His face, to look away, to let him hide. He asks God to "blot out," to erase his iniquity. He doesn't want to look at it anymore and he doesn't want God to look at it anymore. David comes with a broken and contrite heart, naked before God. The repentance is real. But in the agony of exposure David finds forgiveness. Out of that forgiveness comes another Psalm. Now he sings:

> O Lord, Thou hast searched me and known me. Thou dost know when I sit down and when I rise up; Thou dost understand my thought from afar. Thou dost scrutinize my path and my lying down, and art intimately acquainted with all my ways. Even before there is a word on my tongue, behold, O Lord, Thou dost know it all. (Ps. 139:1-4)

In this psalm David acknowledges that there is no refuge from the Spirit of God. Wherever he flees, the Spirit penetrates. No hiding place from the gaze of God is available. David is known and known altogether. Yet the mood of the psalm is not one of lamentation nor even of resignation. No bitterness or frustration can be found in its lines. The psalm is not an expression of fear but of praise and delight. David realizes consolation, not dread, from his awareness of being known. In forgiveness David experiences the benevolent gaze of God and learns what it means to be naked and unashamed. So positive is the experience that once threatened him that David exclaims:

> Search me, O God, and know my heart; try me and know my anxious thoughts; and see if there be any hurtful way in me, and lead me in the everlasting way. (Ps. 139:23-24)

David grasped a lesson that is excruciatingly difficult for the sons of Adam; that being known of God is not the loss of humanity, but the glory of it. He sought relief from the glance of God but could not find it. When he acquiesced to that glance in the pain of repentance, he knew peace.

Like David, those estranged from God behave in a way that often resembles elements of the paranoia syndrome, "The wicked flee when no man pursues"; and as Luther stated, "The pagan trembles at the rustling of a leaf." Like the paranoid who imagines the someone is "out to get him," man lives in terror at the thought of being exposed before God. He imagines that his enemy has but one intent, to destroy him. However, as the paranoid man produces distortions of the enemy, so the guilty man projects upon God the worst of all possible intentions. The design of the gaze of God is to bring repentance and by repentance, life. But here the analogy of the paranoid breaks down. Where the paranoid's enemies are imagined, the divine enemy of the guilty man is real. The threat of judgment is not a charade but an ominous reality when there is no repentance.

To be known of God may mean to be exposed to His wrath. Yet, without it there is no redemption. The experience of Biblical characters is ironic. When they sin, they all fear the gaze of God. When they repent, they all desire to be known of God. In fact, the essence of redemption is understood in terms of being known of God. Christ warned His disciples:

> Not everyone who says to Me, "Lord, Lord," will enter the kingdom of heaven; but he who does the will of My Father who is in heaven. Many will say to Me on that day, "Lord, Lord, did we not prophesy in Your name, and in Your name cast out demons, and in Your name perform many miracles?" And then I will declare to them, "I never knew you; depart from Me, you who practice lawlessness." (Matt. 7:21-23)

The threat of Christ to the hypocrite who uses His name to shield himself from exposure of his moral anarchy is that He will declare him an unknown entity. "I never knew you" is the threat of judgment. In the framework of Christ's understanding, the worst thing that could happen to a man is to be a *stranger* to Him, not to be known by Him. Like the name-dropper who walks up to a celebrity in order to impress his friends only to have the celebrity make it clear that he knows nothing of the man, the hypocrite faces the humiliation of exposure.

Thus, the issue of redemption does not center on the question of whether or not a man "knows" God, but whether or not God "knows" him. To be known of God involves coming out from behind the bushes to experience His benevolent gaze. Thus for the Jew of the Old Testament and the Christian of the New Testament, redemption is tied up with being known of God. The essence of felicity is to be in the presence of the One whose gaze may be terrifying.

One of the most concrete methods of expressing the notion of felicity is contained in the classic Hebrew benediction:

> May the Lord bless you and keep you,
> May He make His face to shine upon you,
> And by gracious unto you.
> May the Lord lift up the light of His countenance
> upon you and give you peace. (Num. 6:24-26)

In this benediction we find a wish expressed in the Hebrew literary form of parallelism. Via parallelism the same basic thought is expressed three times in three different ways. The structure is broken down as follows:

*bless* - - - - - *keep*
make His face to shine - - - - - *gracious*
lift up light of countenance - - - - - peace

The two elements of "blessing" and "keeping" are repeated in synonymous terms. Thus, the blessing is identified with the experience of coming under the gaze of God. To have God make His face shine on you and to lift up the light of His countenance upon you is to know blessedness. For the Jew the highest blessing is to have God look at you, not to overlook you.

A recurring motif of Biblical literature is that motif which draws a parallel between the relationship of God and man and the human situation of marriage. Repeatedly we find the relationship between Israel and Yahweh, Christ and His church, expressed in terms of marriage. Israel is Yahweh's bride as is the New Testament Church the Bride of Christ. Covenant violations and acts of disobedience are described in terms of "adultery," "whoredom," "harlotry," etc. At the heart of the analogy is the concept of "knowing."

When the Old Testament describes the act of sexual intercourse by the verb "to know," it is not being given to euphemism. Abraham *knew* his wife and she conceived. Isaac *knew* his wife.... Likewise, Mary explains in the New Testament, "How can this be since I *know* no man?" Here the word "know" is not being used to express intellectual knowledge or acquaintance of someone. The Old Testament Jew was aware of the facts of biology enough to understand that it took more than an introduction and a handshake to produce children. Mary was not telling the angel that she had never met a man. Rather the term "to know" in this context expresses the zenith of human knowledge, the knowledge of intimacy.

The marriage estate is analogous to the divine-human relationship in many respects. Both involve covenant structures in which the mutual parties are bound to each other by commitment sealed with oaths. Both involve a possibility of knowing-in-intimacy. Both involve a "place" where man can be naked and unashamed. In the context of marriage, I enter into the most intimate of all human relationships. It is a relationship that involves a certain amount of risk. If the marriage is to work, it must involve not only the possibility of my nakedness, but the necessity of it. Within marriage I not only *may* be naked, I must be. If I take the risk and expose myself and discover that my wife has seen my nakedness in all of its ramifications, and still loves me, then I experience at the human level something of what it means to be known of God.

## The Covering of the Naked

Within the Biblical framework there exists not only a concern for nakedness per se, but a concern for the covering of that nakedness as well. We have seen the blessing given to the sons of Noah who covered their father's nakedness. We have seen the startling act of mercy on the part of God when He makes clothes for Adam and Eve. We have noted the mandate of Christ to His disciples to see to it that the naked be clothed. However, the total picture of "covering" transcends these matters of concrete clothing. In Biblical categories of redemption the notion of "covering" takes on far-reaching theological significance.

As the threat of nakedness, of being uncovered, is an ominous warning of judgment, so the promise of salvation is often made in terms of "covering" that exposure. On the one hand we hear the warning of Christ:

> Therefore do not fear them, for there is nothing covered that will not be revealed, and hidden that will not be known. (Matt. 10:26)

This general warning takes on fearful proportions in Jesus' lament over the women of Jerusalem:

> "Daughters of Jerusalem, stop weeping for Me, but weep for yourselves and for your children. For behold, the days are coming when they will say, 'Blessed are the barren, and the wombs that never bore, and the breasts that never nursed.' Then they will begin to say to the mountains, 'Fall on us,' and to the hills, 'Cover us.' " (Luke 23:28-30)

These dreadful warnings of the future state of the unrepentant who will beg for any kind of covering; even that supplied by the shattering of the mountains, is balanced by a promise of a covering for the redeemed.

The Chronicler prays for the "clothing of salvation" (II Chron. 6:41). The prayer of the historian becomes the song of the prophet:

> I will rejoice greatly in the Lord, My soul will exult in my God; for He has clothed me with garments of salvation, He has wrapped me with a robe of righteousness, as a bridegroom decks himself with a garland, and as a bride adorns herself with her jewels. (Isa. 61:10)

The being clothed with righteousness is related in the New Testament to the atonement of Christ. When the righteousness of Christ is imputed to the believer, the believer is no longer naked. Paul alludes to the Pslamist when he writes, "Blessed are those whose lawless deeds have been forgiven, and whose sins have been covered" (Rom. 4:7).

The ultimate "covering" of the believer is anticipated by the Apostle Paul as he contemplates the eschatological status of the redeemed:

> For we know that if the earthly tent which is our house is torn down, we have a building from God, a house not made with hands, eternal in the heavens. For indeed in this house we groan, longing to be clothed with our dwelling from heaven; inasmuch as we, having put it on, shall not be found naked. For indeed while we are in this tent, we groan, being burdened, because we do not want to be unclothed, but to be clothed, in order that what is mortal may be swallowed up by life. (II Cor. 5:1-4)

Here the ultimate hope of the New Testament is expressed—the hope of final covering, of permanent clothing. The hope of the redeemed is to be freed from the threat of nakedness and to enjoy freely the gaze of God.

Kierkegaard understood the "covering dimension" of Christ. He celebrates in passionate terms the covering provided by Christ for His people:

Oh, sure hiding-place for sinners! Oh, blessed hiding-place!—especially if one has first learned what it means when conscience accuses, and the Law condemns, and justice pursues with punishment, and then, when wearied unto despair, to find repose in the one shelter that is to be found! A man, even the most loving man, can at the most give thee extenuation and excuse, leaving it to thee to make what use of them thou art able; but himself he cannot give thee, that only Jesus Christ can do; He gives thee Himself as a shelter; it is not some comforting thought He gives thee, it is not a doctrine He communicates to thee; no, He gives thee Himself. As the night spreads concealment over everything, so did He give up His life and become a covering behind which lies a sinful world which He has saved. Through this covering justice does not break as the sun's rays break through colored glass, merely softened by refraction; no, it impotently breaks against this covering, is reflected from it and does not pass through it. He gave Himself as a covering for the whole world, for thee as well, and for me.[16]

CHAPTER 7

# The Quest for Autonomy

In the early sixties an Anglican Priest arrived in the United States on his first visit to America. Visiting Philadelphia, he spent an afternoon browsing in antique shops taking special note of Revolutionary memorabilia. He was suddenly struck by a time-worn sign hanging in a musty shop bearing the inscription of a Revolutionary War slogan, "We Serve No Sovereign Here!" He found in this experience something that symbolizes an American view of freedom that carries with it an intrinsic repugnance to any notion of sovereign authority. A nation that cherishes liberty above all things, preferring death to its loss, must indeed struggle with any notion that involves absolute sovereignty of anyone, including God. A central motif of the New Testament, "The Kingdom of God," represents a concept alien to basic American thinking. A monarchy, even with Christ on the throne, threatens to some degree our basic principles of democracy.

Perhaps the repugnance to sovereignty that is so integral to the American mentality explains in part the tendency in American church life to relegate Christianity to an isolated "spiritual" or "religious" sphere of national life. There seems to be a process of systematic containment by which the sphere of God's authority is safely restricted to one day in the week and one institution in the culture. To be a nation "under God" does not include the idea that the political leaders are under the authority of God. Separation of Church and State means more than a division of labor between two earthly institutions called to serve God in two different spheres. Rather it means (if meaning of words and phrases can be drawn from customary usage, as Wittgenstein suggests) separation of State and God. Consequently God's authority is limited to the "hearts" of religious people. A political tokenism is manifested when the hats of state are doffed to the Deity in campaign speeches, inauguration ceremonies, special worship services in the White House, and state funerals. Government creeds and public statements openly acknowledge the existence of God, but His sovereign authority is systematically avoided, being relegated to the sphere of the Church. God's sovereignty is not boldly declared at the Watergate Building or in the cloak room of the Senate. The only "Kingdom" our nation would bear would be one that was ruled by referendum. The power of veto does not belong to God. His authority is not sovereign but must be submitted to the tribunal of the popular-opinion poll. The legislation of the United States is not determined by an attempt to reflect divine principles of justice and righteousness but by an attempt to appease lobby groups working to protect vested interests. As Will Durant characterized Aristotle's God as a "Do-nothing" King who reigned but did not rule, so American culture wills a God who reigns but is not Sovereign.

Even within circles of religious evangelism we see an emphasis on the Christ as Saviour rather than on the Christ as Lord. The call to repentance is called an "invitation." Where God sovereignly demands repentance and submission to the authority of His appointed King, the evangelist politely "invites" people to repent. An "invitation" carries with it the right to refuse with impunity. An invitation presents an option not an obligation; an opportunity, not a duty. But God's commands carry no RSVP—man indeed has the power to refuse the divine summons, but not the right.

Thus, within the American culture, the notion of divine sovereignty is short-circuited not only within the "secular" sphere, but in the "religious" sphere as well. God does not rule by executive privilege but must look to the populace to advise and consent. Where Protestant Christiantiy once risked the fracture of all Christian unity over the issue of Sola Scriptura where God's authority in Scripture was to reign supreme, there now exists a profound antipathy to such authority. The seminary professor cries "academic freedom" as the justification for departure from confessional standards, and the church officer appeals to the "living tradition of the Church" as a euphemism for dissolving Biblical mandates. Where the authority of the Apostle Paul was once viewed as an authority that rested upon divine sanction, it is now challenged as being merely the expression of a first century male chauvinist. Paul is viewed as an insufferable obstacle to women seeking "liberation." In a word, modern "liberation" involves a revolt against the sovereign authority of God as members of Church and State join forces in a mutual act of cosmic treason.

When we search for influencing factors which have contributed to the breakdown of respect for divine authority, we must consider the impact of European existentialism upon our culture. Serious work in the area of human freedom and authority has been done by men like Nietzsche, Sartre, Camus, Heidegger and others.

## Nietzsche and Freedom

Nietzsche's conflict with Christianity often focused on Christian morality. At no point in his critique of Christendom did he become more openly hostile than at the point of morality. He saw in the legacy of the "slave-morality" of Christianity the roots of the decadence that plagued his age. He says, "Not their love, but the impotence of their love keeps today's Christians from burning us at the stake." [1] Again he writes, "Christianity gave Eros poison to drink; he did not die of it but degenerated into vice." [2] The Christian ethic with its emphasis on meekness, compassion, etc., has robbed man of the free expression of his will-to-power, producing what Neitzsche calls a "slave-morality." Slave-morality has its roots in a theodicy that seeks consolation in a world without God. Nietzsche maintained the thesis made popular by Dostoevsky: If there is no God, anything is permitted! Paul Roubiczek comments:

> In *The Possessed*, Kirillov is convinced that there is no God, and concludes: "If God exists, all is His will and from His will I cannot escape. If not, it's all my will and I am bound to show self-will. ... If there is no god, then I am God." Or, as Nietzsche puts it: "If there were gods, how could I bear it to be no god myself? Therefore, there are no gods...." Man, deprived of the divine, is bound to reach out for powers once considered divine.[3]

To fill the void of a universe without God, a universe which is characterized by *Das Nichte*, the abyss of nihilism, Neitzsche puts forward the option of "biological heroism." Where there are no values, man must create his own. Freedom is not found in conforming to a slave-morality. Master morality is achieved by the moral pioneer who lives in dialectical courage. His courage is dialectical because, in the final analysis, it is a part of the meaningless Nihil. Nietzche says of the pioneer:

> For, believe me!—the secret of the greatest fruitfulness and the greatest enjoyment of being is: *to live dangerously!* Build your cities on the slopes of Vesuvius! Send your ships into unmapped seas! Live at war with your peers and with yourselves. Be robbers and conquerors, as long as you cannot be rulers and owners, you lovers of knowledge! The time is soon past when it will be enough for you to live hidden like timid deer in the woods. Finally the pursuit of knowledge will stretch out for its due: it will want to *rule* and *possess*, and you along with it.[4]

The pioneer spirit reaches its apex in Nietzsche's figure of the *Übermensch*. The "superman" overcomes and supersedes the present weaknesses of unauthentic man. He does not live in subjection to the heteronomous dictates of Another but in his quest for autonomy, creates his own values. He exchanges the "slave-morality" of decadent Christianity for his own "master morality." There can be no peaceful co-existence between superman and historic Christianity. In Nietzsche's system, the existence of God would be prohibitive for the achieving of authentic existence. The Christian God represents the "Kryptonite" that would be fatal to superman. The Christian God must die lest he continue to castrate the potentially authentic man. We read in *Thus Spake Zarathustra:*

> And this is the great noontide: it is when man stands at the middle of his course between animal and superman and celebrates his journey to a new

morning. . . . Then man, going under, will bless himself; for he will be going over to superman; and the sun of his knowledge will stand at noontide. *"All gods are dead: now we want the superman to live"*—let this be our will one day at the great noontide! [5]

Thus Christianity with its ethic of *theonomy* is on a collision course with man's dream of *autonomy*. If God exists, man cannot be a law unto himself. If God exists, the will-to-power is destined to run head-on into the will of God. God's sovereignty looms as an invincible threat to the aspirations of superman. If man is to be free in the sense of autonomy, then God must die.

Nietzsche's personal attitude toward the existence of God has been the point of countless discussions. Again we find a certain tormented ambivalence in the anguish of Nietzsche's life. At an early age he composed a poem "To the Unknown God" in which he says:

> I must know thee, Unknown One,
> Thou who searchest out the depths of my soul,
> And blowest like a storm through my life.
> Thou are inconceivable and yet my kinsman!
> I must know thee and even serve thee.[6]

In his youth Nietzsche cried out to serve God. It is obvious that this feeling haunted Nietzsche to his grave. His philosophical writings betray a pathetic struggle of "kicking against the ox-goad" that ends in the delusion of self-identity with Christ. He titles his most autobiographical work *Ecce Homo*—"Behold the Man!", borrowing the words Pontius Pilate used to indicate Christ. After his mental breakdown, Nietzsche signed his letters, "the Crucified One." For Frederick Nietzsche the quest for autonomy ended in insanity. He sent his ship into unmapped seas and found shipwreck. He built his house on the slopes of Vesuvius and was consumed by the volcano.

Where Nietzsche presented a passionate, almost poetic study of autonomy, Sartre presents a very analytical study of the question. The principle of subjective volition is at the heart of his understanding of existentialism. In defining what he means by the now famous slogan—"Existence precedes essence," Sartre says:

> Atheistic existentialism, which I represent is more coherent. It states that if God does not exist, there is at least one being in whom existence precedes essence, a being who exists before he can be defined by any concept, and that this being is man, or, as Heidegger says, human reality. What is meant here by saying that existence precedes essence? It means that, first of all, man exists, turns up, appears on the scene, and, only afterwards, defines himself. If man, as the existentialist conceives him, is indefinable, it is because at first he is nothing. Only afterward will he be something, and he himself will have made what he will be. Thus, there is no human nature, since there is no God to conceive it. Not only is man what he conceives himself to be, he is only what he wills himself to be after this thrust toward existence.[7]

For Sartre the first principle of existentialism is that "man is nothing else but what he makes of himself."[8] Man is autonomous. He must choose what he chooses by himself. This involves, of course, an awesome burden of responsibility. In self-choice, man is choosing for all mankind. His decision is not done in isolation. Sartre says:

> In fact, in creating the man that we want to be, there is not a single one of our acts which does not at the same time create an image of man as we think he ought to be.[9]

Sartre is serious about the burden or responsibility that attends decision. It is the burden of God. The loss of God he calls distressing and he has little time for classical humanistic ethics which seek to maintain the values and norms of Christianity without their ultimate foundation—God. Man is free with the absence of God, but this freedom Sartre views as man's condemnation:

> If God does not exist, we find no values or commands to turn to which legitimize our conduct. So, in the bright realm of values, we have no excuse behind us, nor justification before us. We are alone, with no excuses.[10]

At times Sartre seems to celebrate man's freedom in autonomy and at other times, laments it. In his play, *The Flies*, Sartre does not seem so distressed about the absence of God. Rather the God Zeus appears as the menacing threat to human freedom. When Orestes rebels from the "flock" of Zeus, Zeus calls him back by both threatening him with exile if he refuses to return and promising him peace if he does return. Orestes replies:

> Foreign to myself—I know it. Outside nature, against nature, without excuse, beyond remedy, except what remedy I find within myself. But I shall not return under your law; I am doomed to have no other law but mine. Nor shall I come back to nature, the nature you found good; in it are a thousand beaten paths all leading up to you—but I must blaze my trail. For I, Zeus, am a man, and every man must find out his own way. Nature abhors man, and you too, god of gods, abhor mankind.[11]

Here Orestes declares his magna charta. He defies the authority of Zeus. He sees his declaration of autonomy as sealing his own doom. "I am doomed to have no other law but mine." Condemned to be free, Orestes does not delight in his autonomy. But, he prefers the doom of autonomy over submission to Zeus. He may find this freedom unpleasant but not as unpleasant as coming under the rule of Zeus. Zeus is powerless to prevent Orestes' self-emancipation. He shares the "secret of the gods" with Aegistheus:

> Once freedom lights its beacon in a man's heart, the gods are powerless against him. It's a matter between man and man, and it is for other men, and for them only, to let him go his gait, or to throttle him.[12]

For Sartre God represents a threat to authentic morality. If God is autonomous, then man cannot be. By rejecting the existence of God, Sartre makes room for both freedom and morality. Sartre argues that the rejection of God makes morality possible. W. Luijpen, the Dutch Catholic scholar raises the question. "Perhaps it is Sartre's morality that makes the rejection of God necessary." [13]

Although there are decisive differences between Nietzsche and Sartre as well as between Camus, Heidegger, and others, a similar strain of moral autonomy versus the sovereignty of God is evident in all of them. For Heidegger, *Dasein* is authentic only when it manifests itself through self-determination and self-projection. Man, in experiencing the "thrownness" of his existence (*Geworfenheit*), hangs suspended between past and future. To overcome the anxiety that this situation produced, he must carve his own destiny. Authentic existence is characterized by a freedom that can only be maintained apart from heteronomy.[14]

Thus, atheistic existentialism, with its view of autonomous human freedom, places itself on a collision course with Christianity. Its understanding of man makes the God-hypothesis of classical theism untenable. Of course no one can gainsay the argument that the sovereignty of God and the autonomy of man are irreconcilable polar opposites. Here the ubiquitous "dialectic" of contemporary theology cannot function as a translogical *deux ex machina*. Surely the atheist is correct in asserting that human autonomy is incompatible with divine sovereignty.

However, though there is tacit agreement between atheism and historic Christianity at this point, the Christian must go on to pose several questions. Not least is the question whether one can *be* autonomous simply because he declares himself to be. Ultimately, man can be autonomous only if, indeed, there is no God. To argue for the nonexistence of God from the premise that such a God cannot be because man is autonomous, which in turn can be demonstrated only if it is first known that God does not exist, is to argue from the center of a most vicious circle.

Another assertion of atheistic existentialism that remains to be demonstrated is that moral autonomy is a necessary prerequisite for freedom. The fact that man is a volitional being is indeed intrinsic to his being a man and not a thing, a subject and not an object, but must volition be raised to the level of autonomy to be regarded as free?

## Biblical View of Freedom and Autonomy

In Biblical categories of volition, man is created within a framework of freedom, but not antonymy. Man is given freedom, but is refused autonomy. Autonomy belongs to God alone. Man's freedom is within limits. In the Paradise situation he enjoys freedom in the garden but not unlimited freedom. We read:

> The the Lord God took the man and put him into the garden of Eden to cultivate it and keep it. And the Lord God commanded the man, saying,

> "From any tree of the garden you may eat freely; but from the tree of knowledge of good and evil you shall not eat, for in the day that you eat from it you shall surely die." (Gen. 2:15-17)

God places man in a garden paradise. His role is not that of a slave with no freedom or authority but of a king who is given dominion over the earth. Man functions as God's vassal being or viceregent over all creation. Freedom is his—but with one restriction placed upon him. Man is free and responsible. But he is responsible to the law of God.

The Biblical narrative of the Fall rehearses the original quest for autonomy. We read in Genesis 3:

> Now the serpent was more crafty than any beast of the field which the Lord God had made. And he said to the woman, "Indeed, has God said, 'You shall not eat from any tree of the garden'?" And the woman said to the serpent, "From the fruit of the trees of the garden we may eat; but from the fruit of the tree which is in the middle of the garden, God has said, 'You shall not eat from it or touch it, lest you die.' " And the serpent said to the woman, "You surely shall not die. For God knows that in the day you eat from it your eyes will be opened, and you will be like God, knowing good and evil." When the woman saw that the tree was good for food, and that it was a delight to the eyes, and that the tree was desirable to make one wise, she took from its fruit and ate; and she gave also to her husband with her, and he ate. (Gen. 3:1-6)

The seduction scene begins with a "crafty" question, "Did God say?" The serpent raises a question about the limits imposed upon Adam and Eve's freedom. In the very question there is a hint of mockery of the divine command. The implied suggestion is that it was unworthy of God to so restrict His creatures. Luther comments on the text:

Here properly belong these words: "Did God actually command you?" This is an instance of the awful boldness of the devil, as he invents a new god and denies the former true and eternal God with such unconcern and assurance. It is as if he were to say: "Surely you are silly if you believe that God has given such a command, for it is not God's nature to be so deeply concerned whether you eat or not. Inasmuch as it is the tree of the knowledge of good and evil, how can such ill will come upon Him that He does not want you to be wise?" [15]

The integrity of God is called into question by the serpent.

Not only does the serpent raise questions about what God said, but he asks the question in such a way as to distort the commandment. He says, "Has God said, 'You shall not eat from any tree in the garden'?" The serpent obviously knew very well that God had not put the whole garden off limits. The distortion implies the notion that without autonomy there is no freedom. When Eve becomes defensive, protesting their liberty, the serpent becomes boldly direct. He now flatly contradicts the warning of God, saying, "You surely shall not die." The bold and arrogant assertion of the serpent declares to Eve that she can disobey God with impunity. He suggests, like Orestes, that God is "powerless" to carry out His threat. You are responsible to no one is clearly implied in the statement.

Then comes the serpentine promise—the promise of blessing that goes with autonomy—*sicut erat dei*, "you will be as god"! This is the essence of the primordial temptation—to be like God—to have no restraints, no limits, no crowding of self-desire by the rule of another. To be autonomous—that's the temptation.

The irony of humanism which seeks the deification

of man is that it has its origin not in the creed of the ancient Protagoras, *"homo mensura,"* but in the promise of a serpent, *sicut erat dei.* Humanism was not invented by a man, but by a snake who thought the quest for autonomy might be a good idea.

The promise of the serpent was not fulfilled. Adam and Eve did not become gods. Autonomy was not found. What followed was a tragic loss of the freedom previously enjoyed. Human freedom was not augmented, but diminished by the Fall. The quest for autonomy, however, did not cease. It continues even to this day, East of Eden.

The quest for autonomy elucidated in the narrative of the Fall takes on larger dimensions in the mind of the Psalmist. In Psalm 2 the writer envisions a conspiracy not of one man and one woman, but of the aggregate forces of the political kingdoms of this world. The Psalmist asks:

> Why are the nations in an uproar, and the peoples devising a vain thing? The kings of the earth take their stand, and the rulers take counsel together against the Lord and against His Anointed: "Let us tear their fetters apart, and cast away their cords from us!" (Ps. 2:1-3)

The psalm begins with a rhetorical question, a question that suggests amazement at such a manifestation of arrogance and folly. The scene depicts a massive conspiracy to overthrow the authority of God and His Anointed One. (Taken historically the "Anointed" would have reference to the established king of Israel: taken prophetically, to the "Messiah" or the "Christ.") The nations are in a state of tumultuous uproar and are amazed. This rage is manifested in a summit meeting at which the kings and rulers of the world lay aside their paltry differences to join forces against a common enemy. Their border disputes become insignificant as they resolve together to unite their power against the supreme threat—the sovereignty of God.

Why the hostility? Why do the kings rattle their swords in belligerence? The answer is obvious: they despise the rule of God which restricts their freedom. Again the goal is autonomy. The rule of God is regarded as ropes and chains binding them and keeping them from unbridled pursuance of their desire. So the secret weapons are unveiled, the battleships come out of dry dock, the nuclear stockpile is tapped, and the troops are mobilized as the whole world joins the cosmic-liberation movement. With the infantile resolve of the child who seeks to quench a blazing fire with a straw, the rulers set themselves against the sovereignty of God. The response of Yahweh to this revolution is not unconditional surrender; it is not a flurry of actions born of panic; it is not a desperate plea for negotiation in the context of a guarded truce; rather "The one who sits in the heavens laughs . . ." He is temporarily amused by this act of collective insanity. But His laughter turns to anger as He mobilizes His own power to vindicate His Anointed.

Throughout Biblical history we see repeated acts of rebellion to God's sovereign authority. The consequence of these acts is the consequence of the Fall. God punishes with poetic justice. His punishment is in kind. The quest for autonomy produces not liberation, but the loss of freedom. The New Testament describes fallen man as being in bondage—a slave to his own passions.

If ever there is a genuine paradox to be found in Holy Writ, it is at the point of freedom and bondage. The paradox is this: When one seeks to rebel from God, he gains only bondage. When he becomes a slave to God, he becomes free. Liberty is found in obedience.

Jesus provoked the wrath of the Pharisees by saying: "If you abide in My word, then you are truly disciples of Mine; and you shall know the truth, and the truth shall make you free" (John 8:31-32). The offer of freedom by Jesus did not effect a chorus of hosannas. The Pharisees were insulted, arguing that they were already free and hardly needed liberation. Jesus replied, "Truly, truly, I say to you, every one who commits sin is the slave of sin." (John 8:34) Jesus located human slavary in the bondage of the self to its own evil desires. He counters their protestations with the statement, "If therefore the Son shall make you free, you shall be free indeed" (John 8:36).

The Apostle Paul elaborates this theme in his letter to the Romans:

> For if we have become united with Him in the likeness of His death, certainly we shall be also in the likeness of His resurrection, knowing this, that our old self was crucified with Him, that our body of sin might be done away with, that we should no longer be slaves to sin; for he who has died is freed from sin. (Rom. 6:5-7)

Here the Apostle indicates "irreconcilable differences" with the Pharisees. The Pharisees sought freedom by the crucifixion of Christ. Paul found liberty by crucifixion *with* Christ. Paul explains his ironic notion by saying:

> Do you not know that when you present yourselves to someone as slaves for obedience, you are slaves of the one whom you obey, either of sin resulting in death, or of obedience resulting in righteousness? But thanks be to God that though you were slaves of sin, you became obedient from the heart

to that form of teaching to which you were committed, and having been freed from sin, you became slaves of righteousness. (Rom. 6:16-18)

For Paul, there is no liberty in rebellion—only bondage. Liberty is found in obedience in the presence of the Lord. He concludes, "Now the Lord is the Spirit; and where the Spirit of the Lord is, there is liberty" (II Cor. 3:17).

The Biblical God remains a massive threat to illusions of moral autonomy. The result is that even though a man may be convinced of the truth of God's existence, that intellectual assertion in itself could not overcome the moral disinclination to embrace that truth. His corruption is such that he will do everything in his power to disprove, combat, obscure, and deny the truth of that knowledge.

**CHAPTER 8**

# Conclusion

In 1736, in Northampton, Massachusetts, Jonathan Edwards preached a sermon entitled, "Men Are Naturally God's Enemies." In this sermon, Edwards gave a lengthy exposition of the Biblical text, "For if when we were enemies, we were reconciled to God by the death of his son . . . " (Rom. 5:10). The basic thesis of the sermon was that man hated God. Edwards allowed that men rarely claim moral perfection and would readily admit that they sinned. However, men protest the charge that they are enemies of God, arguing that they bear no malice and feel no hatred toward God. Edwards proceeded to challenge that disclaimer by analyzing human behavior in such a way as to demonstrate that man shows his hostility to God by his behavior. Edwards says:

> They are enemies in the natural relish of their souls. They have an inbred distaste and disrelish of God's perfections. God is not such a sort of being as they would have. Though they are ignorant of God, yet from what they hear of him, and from what is manifest by the light of nature of God, they do not like him. By his being endowed with such attributes as he is, they have an aversion to him.

They hear God is an infinitely holy, pure, and righteous Being, and they do not like him upon this account; they have no relish of such kind of qualifications; they take no delight in contemplating them. It would be a mere task, a bondage to a natural man, to be obliged to set himself to contemplate these attributes of God. They see no manner of beauty or loveliness nor taste any sweetness in them. And upon the account of their distaste of these perfections, they dislike all the other of his attributes. They have greater aversion to him because he is omniscient and knows all things; because his omniscience is a holy omniscience. They are not pleased that he is omnipotent, and can do whatever he pleases; because it is a holy omnipotence. They are enemies even to his mercy, because it is a holy mercy. They do not like his immutability, because by this he never will be otherwise than he is, an infinitely holy God.[1]

The thesis of this book is in substantial agreement with Edwards' analysis of man's disposition toward God. In a word, natural man suffers from prejudice. He operates within a framework of insufferable bias against the God of Christianity. The Christian God is utterly repugnant to him because He represents the threat of threats to his own desires and ambitions. The will of man is on a collision course with the will of God. Such a course leads inexorably to a conflict of interests.

There is no dispute with Freud, Nietzsche, etc., on the question of man's ability to create a god according to his own psychological desire or need. This is precisely what Biblical Christianity asserts in the case. There is no dispute that gods so created will reflect the desires of the human creators as Feuerbach maintained. The dispute, of course, is located in the question of whether or not men would be naturally disposed to create the Christian God. Though it is freely acknowledged and granted that man would be pleased to receive the benefits that only God could give them, it is highly questionable whether men desire the God who makes those benefits possible. Men would apparently rather die in their sin than live forever in obedience. They would rather hide behind trees than face the penetrating gaze of God. They would prefer moral anarchy to the law of God.

The writer is grateful to the labor of Marx, Freud, Nietzsche, Sartre, Feuerbach, etc., for their exposé of the idols fabricated by men. In this respect they have done a worthy service to Christianity. Perhaps their iconoclasm will penetrate into those churches which participate in the systematic distortion of the Christian God. So great is the proclivity for idolatry, that even the Christian who knows grace, must continue to struggle against the negative inclinations of his old nature. Can the wholesale attack on the authority of Scripture in our day represent merely the "assured results of higher criticism" or does the modern church betray a gleeful delight in disposing of the weight of Biblical authority? Does the question of the existence of God present problems that are ultimately intellectual or moral?

These questions must be faced before any serious intellectual effort can be made regarding Christian truth claims. I must always ask myself, "Do I believe what I believe because I am honestly persuaded by cogent reasoning that it is true, or do I believe what I believe merely because in the final analysis that's what I want to believe?" If I say I am a Christian, do I believe in the God revealed in Scripture or do I participate in a systematic distortion of that God to suit my own desires? Do I believe in the God who is, or do I believe in a god of my own creation?

The question of the existence of and nature of God is a question attended by a host of vested interests. If we are to examine the question with integrity, we must both recognize and face the implications of our vested interests. If we refuse to do that, then truth will perish, and so will we.

## NOTES TO CHAPTER 1

1. *Webster's New Collegiate Dictionary* (2nd ed.; Springfield: G. & C. Merriam Co., 1956), p. 880.
2. *Ibid.*, p. 355.
3. For a further analysis of the God-talk crisis see, e.g., Edward Farley, *The Transcendence of God* (Phila.: Westminster Press, 1960), and Helmut Gollwitzer, *The Existence of God as Confessed by Faith* (Phila.: Westminster Press, 1965).
4. Paul M. van Buren, *The Secular Meaning of the Gospel* (New York: MacMillan, 1963), p. 3, citing *New Essays in Philosophical Theology*, A. Flew and A MacIntyre, ed. (London: SCM Press, 1955), pp. 96 f.
5. In response to the thesis that the Israelite religion moved in such an evolutionary pattern, see Yehezkel Kaufman, *The Religion of Israel*, trans. Moshe Greenberg (Chicago: University of Chicago Press, 1960).
6. *Early Christian Fathers*, ed. Cyril C. Richardson (*The Library of Christian Classics*, Vol. I; Phila.: Westminster Press, 1953), p. 152.
7. Ernst Cassirer, *The Philosophy of the Enlightenment*, trans. Fritz C. A. Koelln and James P. Pettegrove (Boston: Beacon Press, 1951), p. 134.
8. James Collins, *God in Modern Philosophy* (Chicago: Gateway Edition, 1967), p. 151.
9. *Ibid.*, p. 154.
10. *Ibid.*, pp. 190-200.

11. See John B. Cobb's analysis of Barth in *Living Options in Protestant Theology* (Phila.: Westminster Press, 1962), pp. 171-197.

## NOTES TO CHAPTER 2

1. Wilhelm Windelband, *A History of Philosophy* (New York: Harper & Row, 1958), I, p. 132.
2. Some interpreters of Anselm's classical ontological argument for the existence of God moved in this fashion. For a contemporary discussion of the problem see *The Many-Faced Argument,* eds. John Hick and Arthur C. McGill (New York: MacMillan Co., 1967).
3. This narrow view of verification was propagated by the early school of Logical Positivism. For a broader evaluation of this method of verification see Frederick Ferré's *Language, Logic and God* (New York: Harper & Row, 1961).
4. Irving M. Copi, *Introduction to Logic* (New York: MacMillan Co., 1953).
5. *The Altizer-Montgomery Dialogue* (Chicago: Inter-Varsity Press, 1967), p. 21.

## NOTES TO CHAPTER 3

1. David E. Roberts, *Existentialism and Religious Belief* (New York: Oxford University Press, 1957).
2. Sigmund Freud, *The Future of an Illusion*, trans. W. D. Robson-Scott (New York: Doubleday & Co., 1964), p. 20.
3. *Ibid.*
4. *Ibid.*, p. 22.
5. *Ibid.*, p. 27.
6. See Sigmund Freud, *Civilization and its Discontents*, trans. James Strachey (New York: W. W. Norton & Co., 1961), pp. 21 f.
7. Ludwig Feuerbach, *The Essence of Christianity*, trans. George Eliot (New York: Harper & Row, 1957), p. xxxix.

8. *Ibid.*, p. 135.
9. *Ibid.*, p. 12.
10. *Ibid.*, p. 8.
11. For further analysis of the opium concept see Helmut Gollwitzer's excursus on "Opium des Voekes" (*Die Marxistische Religionskritik und der Christliche Glaube* (Hamburg: Siebenstern Taschenbuch Verlag, 1967) ).
12. Karl Marx, *The Communist Manifesto* (Chicago: Gateway, 1954), p. 35.
13. See Robert N. Beck (ed.), *Perspectives on Philosophy* (New York: Holt, Rinehart and Winston, 1961), p. 370.
14. Hans Joachim Störig, *Geschiedenis van de filosofie*, II (Utrecht: Prisma-Boeken, 1966), p. 254.
15. Friedrich Nietzsche, *Thus Spake Zarathustra*, trans. R. J. Hollingdale (Baltimore: Penguin Books, 1961), p. 42.
16. H. J. Blackham (ed.), *Reality, Man and Existence: Essential Works of Existentialism* (New York: Bantam Books, 1965), p. 71.
17. Bertrand Russell, *Why I am not a Christian* (New York: Simon and Schuster, 1957), p. 22.

## NOTES TO CHAPTER 4

1. John Murray, *The Epistle to the Romans*, Vol. I: *The New International Commentary on the New Testament* (Grand Rapids: Eerdmans, 1959), p. 36.
2. Werner Foerster, "ἀσεβής," *Theological Dictionary of the New Testament*, Vol. VII., eds. Gerhard Kittel and Gerhard Friedrich, trans. Geoffrey W. Bromiley (Grand Rapids: Eerdmans, 1971), p. 190.
3. J. H. Bavinck, *The Church Between the Temple and Mosque* (Grand Rapids: Eerdmans, n. d.), pp. 118-119.
4. Herman Hanse, " κατέχω," *T.D.N.T.*, Vol. II, ed. Gerhard Kittel, trans. Geoffrey W. Bromiley (Grand Rapids: Eerdmans, 1964), p. 829.
5. For a more comprehensive analysis of the historical

debate concerning mediate and immediate general revelation see G. C. Berkouwer, *De Algemene Openbaring*: *Dogmatische Studiën* (Kampen: Kok, 1951), pp. 49-55.

6. Murray, *op. cit.*, pp. 38-39.

7. John Calvin, *Institutes of the Christian Religion*, Vol. I, trans. Henry Beveridge (Grand Rapids: Eerdmans, 1964), p. 57.

8. *Ibid.*, p. 62.

9. David W. Torrance and Thomas F. Torrance (eds.), *The Epistles of Paul the Apostle to the Romans and to the Thessalonians*, Vol. VIII of *Calvin's Commentaries*, trans. Ross MacKenzie (Grand Rapids: Eerdmans, 1961), p. 31.

10. Rudolf Bultmann writes, "Thus in the concept of the knowledge of God the element of knowledge emerges alongside and sometimes prior to that of acknowledgment. The two are obviously linked in R. 1:18-23 (esp. 21). "γινώσκω," *T.D.N.T.*, Vol. I, p. 205.

11. George Bertram, "μωρός," *T.D.N.T.* Vol. IV, p. 832.

12. Murray, *op. cit.*, p. 41.

13. Mircea Eliade, *The Sacred and Profane*, trans. William R. Trask (New York: Harper & Row, 1957), pp. 122-123.

14. *Ibid.*

15. Karl Barth, *The Epistle to the Romans*, trans. 6th ed., Edwyn C. Hoskyns (London: Oxford University Press, 1933), p. 51.

16. Wilhelm Pauck (ed.), *Luther: Lectures on Romans* Vol. XV of *The Library of Christian Classics*, eds. John Baille, John T. McNeill, and Henry P. Van Dusen (Phila.: Westminster, 1961), p. 33.

17. J. A. C. Van Leeuwen adds, "De zonde van het heidendom is, dat het den waarachtigen God heeft laten varen, en in Zÿne plaats de afgoden gesteld, dat zÿ het schepsel eer bewezen en dienden, en Gode de eer onthielden, die Hem alleen toekomt." *Romeinen: Korte Verklaring Der Heilige Schrift* (Kampen: Kok, 1932), p. 19.

18. See *Leviticus* 18:22-30, 20:13.

19. Paul develops this moral aspect of general revela-

tion in the second chapter of *Romans*.
20. Murray, *op. cit.*, p. 53.
21. *Webster's New Collegiate Dictionary*, p. 904.
22. Calvin, *Institutes*, Vol. I, pp. 38-39.
23. *Webster's New Collegiate Dictionary*, p. 719.
24. Bavinck, *op. cit.*, p. 121.
25. *Ibid.*, p. 122.
26. Helmut Gollwitzer, *The Existence of God as Confessed by Faith*, trans. James W. Leitch (Phila.: Westminster, 1965), pp. 89 f.

## NOTES TO CHAPTER 5

1. Eliade, *The Sacred and Profane*, p. 8.
2. Rudolf Otto, *The Idea of the Holy*, trans. John W. Harvey (New York: Oxford University Press, 1958).
3. *Ibid.*, p. 7.
4. Otto sharply distinguishes between what he means by creature-feeling and Schleiermacher's notion of "feeling of dependence" and is critical of William James' analysis in *Varieties of Religious Experience*.
5. Otto, *op. cit.*, p. 10.
6. *Ibid.*, p. 14.
7. Geerhardus Vos, *Biblical Theology* (Grand Rapids: Eerdmans, 1948), p. 96. Cf. Edmond Jacob, *Theology of the Old Testament*, trans. Arthur W. Heathcote and Philip J. Allcock (New York: Harper & Brothers, 1958), p. 47.
8. Eliade, *op. cit.*, p. 9.
9. Otto, *op. cit.*, p. 23.
10. *Ibid.*, p. 31.
11. Calvin, *Institutes*, I, p. 39, (italics mine).
12. Vos, *op. cit.*, p. 267.
13. John H. Gerstner, *Reasons for Faith* (New York: Harper & Brothers, 1960), p. 81.
14. Laurence J. Peter and Raymond Hull, *The Peter Principle* (New York: Bantam Books, 1969), p. 28.
15. John Steinbeck, *Of Mice and Men* (New York: Modern Library, 1937), p. 158.
16. Jacob, *Theology of the Old Testament*, pp. 79-80.

17. Gerhard Kittel, "δόξα," *T.D.N.T.*, Vol. II, p. 238.
18. *Ibid.*
19. *Ibid.*, p. 248.

## NOTES TO CHAPTER 6

1. W. Luijpen, *Fenomenologie en Atheisme* (Utrecht: Aula-Boeken, 1967), p. 33.
2. Jean-Paul Sartre, *Being and Nothingness*, trans. Hazel E. Barnes (New York: Washington Square Press, 1953), p. 319.
3. *Ibid.*, p. 354.
4. *Ibid.*, p. 355.
5. Jean-Paul Sartre, *No Exit and Three Other Plays* (New York: Vintage Books, 1949), p. 47.
6. *Ibid.*
7. Julias Fast, *Body Language* (New York: M. Evans & Co., 1970), p. 140.
8. Desmond Morris, *The Naked Ape* (New York: Dell, 1967), p. 9.
9. Søren Kierkegaard, *Either/Or*, Vol. II, trans. Walter Lowrie (Garden City: Anchor Books, 1959), p. 163.
10. *Ibid.*, p. 164.
11. Søren Kierkegaard, *Fear and Trembling and The Sickness unto Death*, trans. Walter Lowrie (Garden City: Doubleday Anchor Books, 1954), pp. 197-198.
12. S. U. Zuidema, *Kierkegaard*, trans. David H. Freeman (Phila.: Presbyterian & Reformed Pub. Co., 1960), p. 20.
13. Albrecht Oepke, "γυμνός ," *T.D.N.T.*, Vol. I., p. 774.
14. Martin Luther, *Lectures on Genesis*, Vol. I of Luther's Works, ed. Jaroslav Pelikan (Saint Louis: Concordia Publishing House, 1958), p. 167.
15. Sartre, *Being and Nothingness*, p. 354.
16. Robert Bretall (ed.), *A Kierkegaard Anthology* (New York: The Modern Library, 1936), pp. 424-425.

## NOTES TO CHAPTER 7

1. Houston Peterson (ed.), *Essays in Philosophy* (New York: Pocket Books, 1959), p. 220.

2. *Ibid.*, p. 228.
3. Paul Roubiczek, *Existentialism For and Against* (Cambridge: Cambridge University Press, 1964), p. 32.
4. Robert N. Beck (ed.), *Perspectives in Philosophy* (New York: Holt, Rinehart and Winston, 1961), p. 371.
5. Neitzsche, *Thus Spake Zarathustra*, p. 104.
6. Cited by William Barrett, *Irrational Man* (Garden City: Doubleday Anchor Books, 1958), p. 186.
7. Beck, *op. cit.*, p. 364.
8. *Ibid.*
9. *Ibid.*
10. *Ibid.*, p. 366.
11. Sartre, *No Exit and Three Other Plays*, p. 122.
12. *Ibid.*, p. 104.
13. Luijpen, *Fenomenologie en Atheisme*, p. 326.
14. Cf. my "Existential Autonomy and Christian Freedom," *Christianity Today*, July 18, 1969, p. 13.
15. Luther, *Lectures on Genesis*, p. 149.
16. Albert Cook (ed.), *Augustine: Confessions and Enchiridion*, Vol. VII of *The Library of Christian Classics*, eds. John Baille, John T. McNeill, and Henry P. Van Dusen (Phila.: Westminster, 1953), p. 357.
17. Cf. Adolf Harnack, *History of Dogma* Vols. IV & V, trans. Neil Buchanan (New York: Dover Publications, 1961), pp. 204-217.
18. Martin Luther, *The Bondage of the Will*, trans. J. I. Packer and O. R. Johnston (Westwood: Fleming H. Revell, 1957), p. 265.
19. *Ibid.*
20. *Ibid.*, p. 137.
21. *Ibid.*, p. 162.
22. *Ibid.*, p. 104.
23. *Ibid.*, p. 103.
24. *Ibid.*, p. 220.
25. John Calvin, *Institutes* Vol. I, p. 181.
26. *Ibid.*, p. 253.
27. *Ibid.*, p. 254.
28. Jonathan Edwards, *Freedom of the Will*, ed. Paul Ramsey (New Haven: Yale University Press, 1957), p. 137.
29. *Ibid.*, p. 146.
30. *Ibid.*, p. 159.

## NOTES TO CHAPTER 8

1. Jonathan Edwards, *The Works of President Edwards* Vol. IV (New York: Robert Carter and Brothers, 1879), p. 38.

# Index of Names

Aristotle, 13, 28, 29, 31, 35, 138

Barth, Karl, 24, 69, 78
Bavinck, J. H., 59, 60, 73, 76, 78
Bertram, George, 66
Bultmann, Rudolph, 24, 79

Calvin, John, 58, 62, 63, 74, 75, 78, 79, 88-90
Camus, Albert, 140, 145
Cassirer, Ernst, 20, 21
Cicero, 35

Descartes, Rene, 35
d'Holbach, Paul Henri Thiry, 21, 22
Diderot, Denise, 21, 22
Dostoevsky, Fyodor, 140
Durant, Will, 138

Edwards, Jonathan, 153, 154
Eliade, Mircea, 68, 81, 85

Fast, Julius, 111, 112
Feuerbach, Ludwig, 44-46, 48, 53, 79, 155

Flew, Anthony, 14, 15
Freud, Sigmund, 23, 42-44, 48, 50-53, 59, 77, 79, 95, 154, 155

Gerstner, John, 97
Gollwitzer, Helmut, 80

Handrian, 118
Heidegger, Martin, 140, 143, 145
Herder, J. G., 22
Hollander, Xaviera, 41
Hume, David, 35, 52

Jaspers, Karl, 24

Kant, Immanuel, 22, 23, 35, 52
Kierkegaard, Soren, 54, 83, 114-118, 135, 136
Kittel, Gerhard, 58, 103, 105

Leary, Timothy, 38
Lessing, G., 22
Luijpen, W., 145
Luther, Martin, 69, 70, 125, 130, 147, 148

Marx, Karl, 23, 46-48, 50, 53, 54, 79, 155
Mill, John Stewart, 35
Montgomery, John Warwick, 39
Morris, Desmond, 113
Murray, John, 58, 61, 68, 72

Nietszche, Friedrich, 15, 23, 47, 48, 54, 55, 73, 140-143, 154, 155

Otto, Rudolf, 81-89

Pascal, Blaise, 41, 42
Plato, 13
Polycarp, 17

Protagoras, 149

Roubiczek, Paul, 140
Russell, Bertrand, 48, 49

Sartre, Jean-Paul, 107-110, 118, 124-126, 140-, 143-145, 155
Shaw, George Bernard, 97
Steinbeck, John, 100-102

Tillich, Paul, 80

Vos, Geerhardus, 92

Wittgenstein, Ludwig, 138

Zuidema, S. U., 117